Pas de Deux

Linda Boulton

Pas de Deux
A Carer's Story

For Sally and Katie

Pas de Deux: A Carer's Story
ISBN 978 1 76109 139 1
Copyright © Linda Boulton 2021
Cover image: Green Leaves Studio

First published 2021 by
GINNINDERRA PRESS
PO Box 3461 Port Adelaide 5015
www.ginninderrapress.com.au

In memory of Stephen Russell Boulton

Contents

Entrée	9
Adagio	11
Male Variation	21
Female Variation	61
Coda	129
Curtain Call	159
Acknowledgements	168

Entrée

We stand on a darkened stage, the curtain closed. The audience is hushed and waiting in anticipation. I hear the strains of the introduction and Ludwig Minkus's *Don Quixote* fills the theatre with its magnificence. The music builds and my heart flutters. With a few last-minute adjustments to my costume, I stand *en pointe*, feeling the tips of my toes pressing into the familiar hardness of my ballet shoes. My partner and I prepare for a supported pirouette, a series of turns effortlessly achieved as the male dancer supports the ballerina in multiple spins. I feel his hands at my waist, turning me, straightening me when I threaten to go off-balance, pulling me upright. We try again and this time it is perfect. We move together with ease, synchronicity and poise.

It is almost time. We assume our starting position. We stand together, our feet in fifth position, arms in *bras bas*. It is a simple pose that belies the difficulty of the *pas de deux* we are about to perform. I will balance precariously on tiptoe and glide across the stage; he will leap and soar through the air. He will lift me effortlessly and I will feel safe in his arms. It is a perfect partnership, this blend of grace and strength.

The curtain opens and the spotlight finds us. I am dressed in a simple red tutu, a rose pinned behind my ear. He is resplendent in black tights and bolero, white shirt and red cummerbund. We are alone, together, in a halo of light, about to enter a glorious world of movement and music.

Adagio

We met in a dance studio when we were seventeen. Ballet had been my passion since childhood and I'd just opened a dancing school but Steve was a late starter. Someone had told him that ballet would improve his football skills, but football was soon forgotten. He was instantly smitten and his physique and flexibility made him a promising ballet student.

Steve was tall and lanky with long curly hair parted down the middle. He was 'Curly' to his family and close friends, and later, when admired for his ballet and athletic skills, was nicknamed 'Flash' by his work colleagues. Regular childhood sunburns had left Steve's fair skin freckled. He wore gold-rimmed John Lennon glasses and drove a bright blue Holden FJ. He reminded me of Aunty Jack, a TV character of the 1970s.

Steve had a carefree childhood filled with beach holidays, swimming, boating and fishing. A photo from the time shows a bare-chested, freckled youngster with a big smile and a mop of curls proudly posing with a freshly caught fish. Steve was athletic and loved all sports. Ballet provided yet another outlet in which he could express his energy, enthusiasm and physical prowess. It was also an art form that married athletic ability with grace and beauty – a combination that was intoxicating to Steve and which would become a lifelong infatuation.

After finishing Year 12, Steve enrolled in an industrial arts course at teacher's college but withdrew from his studies six months later. His parents were unable to support him and he needed money. He found a job as a bank teller and began saving to complete his education while at the same time attending ballet classes. Newcastle, although renowned for its steelworks, also produced a high standard of dancer, with many local ballet students pursuing professional careers in ballet companies both in Australia and overseas.

By the age of twenty, ballet had become Steve's focus and he was ambitious. When a male teacher, a former dancer with the Royal Ballet, opened a ballet school in Newcastle, we both joined his classes. Our teacher formed an amateur dance group and we began performing regularly, dancing the traditional *pas de deux* from all the famous ballets. Our ballet partnership blossomed into romance and we became inseparable. We were together for ballet classes most days of the week and rehearsals at weekends.

We'd been a couple for five years when, in December 1979, Steve packed his bags and flew to Europe for the Christmas holidays. By then, he was working as a high school teacher but his dream was to join a ballet company. This trip was to seek job opportunities overseas. I watched in tears as his small plane took off from a local airport and disappeared into the bright blue summer sky. I was wearing a red T-shirt and Steve later told me he'd looked down from the aircraft until I'd become a small red speck in the distance.

Steve watched Nureyev rehearse in Paris, went to Covent Garden in London, and did classes with a ballet company in Austria. For six weeks, he toured Europe and I stayed at home alone wondering if he would come back to me.

Then, one night in late January, I looked out of the kitchen window and saw his blue Holden coming up the drive. He stood before me looking tired and thin after his travels but he'd made his decision and was happy to be home. Within days, we were engaged, and four months later we were married.

In the days leading up to the wedding, a storm raged and, as the gale force winds blew and it teemed with rain, I became increasingly nervous. The weather matched my mood and I was plagued with doubts. Suddenly, I wondered if we really suited. We had grown up in such different homes. My parents were European and conservative; his were Aussie battlers, a little rough around the edges, and living in an old miner's cottage with a wood-fire stove in the kitchen and gaps in the add-on bathroom that were so wide the cold wind whistled through them in winter. I worried that my parents disapproved of Steve's family, although nothing was ever said.

Steve's parents, Collin and Jean, had met on Flinders Street, Melbourne, during the war. One night, while out on the town, Jean and a friend spied two servicemen walking towards them. The men, handsome in their uniforms, must have impressed the girls, because Jean nudged her friend and pointed to the young Collin. 'I'll have him!' Collin walked her home that night and so began a romance that spanned almost seven decades. They married on 1 February 1945 in a Melbourne church. Jean was seventeen and Collin was twenty and there was a baby on the way. Years later, and after the birth of their fourth child, Steve, they moved to Newcastle where Col had grown up.

Steve was six when the family arrived in Newcastle. His parents bought a corner shop in New Lambton which Jean ran for ten years. Col was a car mechanic but retired when he suffered a neck injury at work. Later, they sold the shop and lived on the pension. Steve's two older brothers became car mechanics and his sister found work in a laundry. Steve was different. He rejected the traditional male roles the men in the family occupied and pursued his own interests, particularly dance, with fervour and enthusiasm. Although their financial support was limited, the family allowed him the freedom to explore his passion for dance without criticism and were always proud of his academic and dance achievements.

The night before the wedding, we gathered at Steve's parents' house. Relatives had arrived from interstate and I sat next to his grandmother, a portly little lady with permed white hair and a no-nonsense manner. She'd outlived two husbands, given birth to eight children, worked as a nurse's aide in her later years and was currently keeping company with a gentleman named Bert.

I had never known my own grandparents. When my family migrated to Australia from The Netherlands, they left behind parents, siblings and cousins, an extended family that my brothers, sister and I never got to know. I was thrilled to finally have a grandmother figure and was very fond of Nan. Now I confided my fears.

'It's just last-minute nerves, dear,' she said, but I wasn't reassured. She patted my hand as I wiped away my tears.

I couldn't cancel the wedding now. Everything was ready for the big day – dress made, venue booked, catering organised.

Our wedding day, 10 May 1980, dawned sunny and clear. The storm had passed and so had my fears. When we arrived at the church, I held onto my father's arm and prepared to walk down the aisle. I stood in the late afternoon sunlight of a beautiful autumn day as my bridesmaids arranged my gown and veil. Then, in through the doors of the church as the organist began playing, I saw Steve standing at the altar, waiting for me.

Someone filmed us as we left the church and posed for photos in the grounds. It is a grainy forty-millimetre film – no sound, just images captured in time. Steve's dad, full-faced and in his prime, is joking around with his sisters-in-law. Steve's mother, unhappy with her hairstyle that day, has a pinched look on her face. I see my father's crooked smile and my mother chatting animatedly. A group of my ballet students flit into and out of camera range.

I am wearing an elegant cream gown, lace-edged and pearl-encrusted. Steve stands straight and tall in his beige suit and maroon bow tie. I gaze up adoringly at my new husband and he puts his arm protectively around my waist. We pose for the camera, our smiling faces radiating through the years. I look calm and poised, Steve happy and proud.

We watched the home movie one Christmas with our daughters, Sally and Katie, and their partners. They laughed at the 1980s fashions and the antics of their young cousins. But they also looked on in wonder, mesmerised by the footage of their parents. We were young, vibrant, healthy and whole.

*

Sally, our firstborn, arrives on a June night in 1984. She is tiny but perfect and Steve is besotted. Someone takes a photo of him that night in the nursery with his new daughter cradled in his arms. She is swaddled in a flannelette blanket, her little head poking out from the folds, her eyes wide open. They are standing in front of a poster of a duckling nestled in a denim shirt pocket. The inscription on the poster reads, 'Lord, protect me and keep me close to your heart.' When he leaves the hospital at midnight, he goes home and rings all our friends to tell them about his beautiful baby girl.

I am exhausted from the birth and a difficult pregnancy marked by constant nausea. In the following days, I am weak and unwell and feel little emotion for my baby. When I come home from hospital, I gently place her in the bassinet and look down at her, overwhelmed by this new responsibility. How will I ever look after her? Sometimes I stand in the shower and weep, despondent over my apparent lack of maternal love. But as the weeks turn into months, a bond develops.

On my first day back at work, when Sally is three months old, I take her to her grandparents. I see my father bouncing her on his knee, a little cherub in a pink grow-suit, and I know I don't want to leave her. When Katie is born four years later, I bond with her instantly. She nestles into my neck like a little koala bear and our family is complete.

*

April 2001. It is a beautiful autumn day. The sun's rays still hold warmth, although the air is crisp and clear. Our family is on a bush walk. Steve and our daughters run on ahead. We begin a steep incline, our feet crushing the fallen leaves underfoot. Steve lags behind. Striding ahead, I glance back over my shoulder and see him slowly negotiating the rough track. I notice that his right arm isn't swinging as he walks. A small flutter of fear floats nearby, but I push it resolutely away. Then I remember other barely perceptible changes – the way his foot sometimes drags a little when he walks, the disturbed sleep when his body twitches restlessly in the night. The sound of my heart beating breaks the deafening silence. In the distance, a bird caws. Above me, the sun passes behind a cloud. The day has suddenly turned cold.

*

23 August 2001. It starts like any other day: morning showers, breakfast, school lunches made, children dropped at school. By eleven a.m., we are ready to leave for the midday appointment. Steve has been referred to a neurologist for a nerve conduction test on his troublesome arm. He is nervous. I notice that his hands are shaking and I'm surprised at this rare show of anxiety. I hope he never gets anything serious wrong with him, I think. He'd never cope. I tell him to relax, that everything will be fine, but he isn't convinced.

We park in Hunter Street near the Star Arcade, across the road from the TAFE. The old buildings stand as silent witnesses as we lock the car and put money in the meter. It is a cold morning, the arcade a wind tunnel. We are buffeted by strong gusts as we make our way down the almost deserted passageway. An old homeless man sits huddled in a corner and I avert my eyes. I have my own, more pressing, concerns.

The waiting room is like doctors' waiting rooms the world over. The walls and carpet are in neutral hues of beige and grey and we perch nervously on hard blue chairs. I see a stand in the corner of the room with pamphlets describing all kinds of diseases. I glance over them but the subject matter is too confronting – MS, Parkinson's, motor neurone disease. None of these apply to us, surely. An advertisement for a Parkinson's support group hangs on the wall. I am suddenly acutely aware that we are in a neurologist's waiting room.

Soon, the doctor ushers us in and sits at his wooden desk. We sit on two chairs facing him and answer his questions about Steve's medical history. Then he performs a complete neurological examination, one we become only too familiar with in the coming months and years. Partway through, Steve asks if he is passing the test. It is his attempt at humour, to hide his nervousness, but the doctor doesn't bite. Instead, he says something I don't want to hear.

'There are some motor function problems.'

Before long, the examination is over and Steve is seated on the edge of the examination table.

'Do you know what's wrong with me?' he asks, and the doctor replies without hesitation.

'I think you have early onset Parkinson's disease.'

Steve's face turns white and he needs to lie down.

I begin to shake and can't stop. 'But isn't he too young for Parkinson's?' I plead. 'He's only forty-six.'

The doctor shakes his head and tells us people in their twenties and thirties can develop it. Then he looks at me and asks, 'Haven't you noticed Steve's expressionless face?'

But I haven't noticed any changes.

Somehow we struggle from that dreadful room and, armed with referrals for blood tests and an MRI, find our way back to our car. We are inconsolable but, inconceivably, nothing has changed since we entered the doctor's rooms an hour earlier. The homeless man is still sitting in his corner and the wind is still blowing down that desolate arcade.

We drive to Bar Beach car park and sit looking out over the pounding waves of the winter surf. But we are oblivious to the spectacular surroundings. I keep replaying the doctor's words in my head. I can't believe the diagnosis. Surely the doctor has made a mistake. How can Steve possibly have a neurological disease? He is hardly ever sick and seems fit and healthy in every way. He doesn't even have a tremor.

I soon learn that Steve has already lost eighty per cent of the dopamine-producing cells in his brain and that he has, in fact, already been displaying Parkinson's symptoms without either of us realising. I think about the arm that doesn't swing as he walks, and the way his foot drags. I think about the sleep problems and the jerking and twitching that so disturbs my sleep. Then I remember how our dance teacher would tell Steve to put some expression in his face when he was performing, how his mouth would be open and his eyes would be staring 'like a dead fish'. But that was back in his twenties. Surely, he couldn't have had Parkinson's for that long?

We go back to our GP that afternoon and he, too, is surprised by the diagnosis. He is sympathetic and tries to be reassuring. Steve asks him how long he'll be able to continue working. The doctor suggests ten years, a figure that we now know would have been impossible to predict. Every individual's progression of the disease is different, and there is no way of knowing how fast a patient will deteriorate. Still, the doctor's words that day are comforting because Steve is concerned about his ability to continue providing for his family. If he can work for several more years at least, our financial status will remain stable.

We decide not to tell our children that day and wait until further tests confirm the diagnosis. When we do tell them, they react in different ways. We are despondent but Sally, at seventeen, displays a maturity beyond her years.

'Someone's got to stay strong,' she says bravely.

Katie, at thirteen, rails against the news. 'Isn't that what Michael J. Fox has got?' she weeps, knowing instinctively the implications of the diagnosis.

Steve refuses to tell his colleagues about the diagnosis. He confides in one teacher friend so that he will have some level of support at school but keeps the news about his illness hidden from the head staff. He fears repercussions and questions about his ability to continue working. It will, in fact, be three years before his illness becomes public, and then only because he is hospitalised for a psychosis.

So we both keep the diagnosis a secret, hidden from all except a select few. The price we pay for hiding the news means that we are unable to share our distress. We pretend that nothing is wrong although we are both terrified of what the future holds. Steve refuses to read anything about Parkinson's and dislikes talking about his condition. He holds it at arm's length although each new symptom induces panic. I weep daily for weeks and months until one day I realise I haven't cried all day. I am beginning to adjust to this third party in our marriage.

A friend gives us a printout on Parkinson's disease. Steve won't look at it but, some months after his diagnosis, I find the courage to start reading. The article describes the stages of the disease and, after the first page I put it away. I'm not ready to face the facts either.

Later, I attend a Parkinson's support group. Steve refuses to come with me, so I go alone. I sit for a while in the car park and watch people enter the community hall. Most are elderly, some on walkers. When I introduce myself to the woman recording attendance, my eyes fill and she puts her arms around me. A middle-aged woman comes towards us. Her body jerks in uncontrollable writhing movements as she speaks to me. She tells me she has had Parkinson's for many years and that several other members of her family also suffer from the condition. She is bright and optimistic but I cringe away from her obvious disability.

Later, I find a seat at the end of a row away from the other group members. An official panel sit at a table at the front of the room and discuss housekeeping matters. Then an elderly man puts the group through some simple exercises. They have a guest speaker today, an occupational therapist, but I hardly hear a word she says. When the meeting ends, and tea and coffee are served, I slip out of the hall and run back to the safety of my car.

We rely on medication to control the symptoms and pray the disease will progress slowly. Steve functions reasonably well at this early stage but he is never satisfied. He wants more from the drugs, craving a quick fix and a return to normalcy. His medication is increased to enable him to keep working and includes Cabaser, a drug that mimics the action of levodopa. Levodopa, a dopamine replacement, is urgently needed now that Steve's brain is not producing enough dopamine naturally. Later, he is introduced to Sinemet (one of the main levodopa treatments for Parkinson's) but this is delayed for as long as possible because of its unwanted side effects, particularly the unwelcome dyskinesia, or involuntary movements, that commonly occur after its extended use.

*

Steve is the creative arts coordinator at school, a position he coveted and worked hard to obtain. With his love of theatre and dance and easy rapport with staff and students alike, he is a popular choice for the role. Under his guidance, the school wins a local rock eisteddfod, and presents annual musicals such as *Oliver* and *My Fair Lady*. Steve is in his element and thrives on the buzz and adulation over the success of these amateur productions.

When the coordinator position comes up for renewal three years after his diagnosis, Steve goes through the process of reapplying. I need to help him with his application – clearly his writing and communication skills are faltering – but we press on. I'm not surprised when he is unsuccessful but it is a cruel blow to Steve's self-esteem. By now, his diagnosis has been made public and teachers are noticing a problem – Steve is not performing well.

My own career is suffering too. After Steve's diagnosis, my already waning interest in the ballet school plummets even further. Over the years, class sizes have decreased and the new intake of students seems to diminish with each successive year. I have been teaching ballet for some thirty years and have become tired, jaded and disheartened with the job and the lack of numbers and capacity for the school to grow. Now the prospect of dealing with Steve's illness, while at the same time managing a business, seems overwhelming. At the end of 2001, I send a letter to my students telling them of my decision to hand my school over to a former pupil. She will manage the dancing school and I will teach some classes for her. This relieves me of the onerous duty of preparing and organising the annual concert and other tasks that come with the managerial role. I do not divulge Steve's illness or the reasons for my decision.

Relinquishing my ballet school is heart-wrenching, and the first twelve months are filled with grief, angst and regret. I know almost immediately that I have made the wrong decision. I question and berate myself constantly. I worry about the students and how they are coping. I know many of the girls and their mothers are unhappy about the changes but most stay loyal to me; I have nurtured and fostered these students since they were small and my bond with them is strong. The wider implications of Steve's illness on my identity are also emerging. The long-held role I had once performed with ease is now redundant, and the loss of control and sense of dislocation adds to my distress. I want my old life back, before Steve became ill and our normal routines were so devastatingly interrupted.

Male Variation

August 2004. Steve is sitting on the lounge room floor surrounded by papers – bank statements, bills, receipts and miscellaneous paperwork that I'd forgotten even existed. The interrogation begins.

'Where's the money? Why have you opened up another account in your name?'

He doesn't believe me when I deny any wrongdoing. He thinks that I am taking all our money and leaving him. He finds receipts from an overseas trip we made nine years earlier and thinks I am going to America. I cannot convince him that these papers are dated from years before, that they are no longer valid, and that I have no intention of travelling anywhere. I am frightened. My father, in the throes of Alzheimer's disease, had acted in a similar way, paranoid about Telstra taking his money. He, too, had littered the house with paperwork. Steve's behaviour brings back painful memories and I know something is seriously wrong.

Last night, he accused me of having an affair. He was calm but icy. There was no anger but a chilling disappointment in me, and disbelief that I would betray him. He had looked for evidence of my infidelity checking my emails, phone and even my underwear.

I tried to reassure him that his allegations were nonsense but he'd left, taken the car and disappeared for hours.

Returning late at night, he climbed into bed and we lay together in silence. Then, after breaking the stillness with a measured tone, 'I can't believe you would do that to me,' he turned away from me and went to sleep.

This morning, I run from the littered room. I am frantic. I arrive at the doctor's surgery crying and barely coherent. The secretary, seeing my distress, ushers me into a back room and the doctor comes in soon after. He tells me that he thinks Steve's behaviour is due to medication and not the onset of dementia as I had feared. He says he will ring the neurologist to ask for advice, and an antipsychotic is prescribed.

The following day, Steve asks Sally to check details about his medication and we turn on the computer. He is suspicious about the drugs now and is sure that the doctors are in on a conspiracy with the drug company. Then he sees a letter from Myer and insists they know intimate details about us. Sally becomes upset by this stranger, her father, who is behaving so erratically. Somehow, she convinces him to close the computer and escapes to her bedroom. I ring the doctor's surgery and am told to bring him down. Luckily, he likes his GP and agrees to go with me.

In the car, I feel the beginnings of a migraine. Zigzag patterns dance in front of my eyes. We make it to the doctor before the encroaching blindness of the aura makes driving impossible. I am given an injection for the migraine and the doctor talks to Steve about the strange thoughts he is having. They discuss the unlikelihood of an affair and of me absconding with all the money. The doctor reassures Steve about the reliability of his medications. Steve is surprisingly compliant and agreeable. The doctor tells me to bring him back each day so that he can monitor the symptoms and provide me with some support until we can see the neurologist.

A friend has given us tickets to the ballet *Swan Lake*. Steve seems calmer this evening; perhaps the performance will provide a pleasant distraction for him. I drop him off at the Civic Theatre and then search for a parking spot. By the time I arrive back at the theatre, Steve is agitated. He asks me why I've taken so long. Then he grills me about an orange car he 'saw' me getting into. I manage to pacify him and we join the throng entering the auditorium. I feel suddenly claustrophobic and need to resist the urge to flee the crowded foyer. We take our seats and soon Tchaikovsky's famous music fills the theatre, the curtain lifts, and the dancers move gracefully across the stage. Beside me, Steve is restless.

He cannot concentrate on the performance and wants to get up out of his seat. The ballerinas in their white tutus blur in front of my tear-filled eyes. When the curtain comes down for interval, I take him home.

Later, in the early hours of the morning, Steve jumps out of bed, runs out of the house and stands on the front lawn. It is cold, and he is barefoot in his boxer shorts and T-shirt. He refuses to come back inside despite my desperate pleas. He is convinced I am leaving him and is waiting for the 'orange car' to come and pick me up. He tells me to turn off all the lights in the house. When I turn on the light to use the bathroom, he accuses me of signalling my lover. Our daughters are awake by now and between us we decide I should ring the ambulance. Steve hears me making the call and gets in his car and drives off into the darkness. The girls and I wait anxiously, praying that he will be safe. A short time later, I hear his car turn into the drive. Steve comes inside with a slight smirk on his face but says nothing. Instead, he heads for the bedroom, climbs into bed and instantly falls asleep.

Steve is admitted to hospital a few days later when a bed becomes available. He goes willingly because the newly prescribed antipsychotic has affected his Parkinson's symptoms and he is having difficulty with his mobility. My previously agile husband is now a shuffling, drooling specimen, almost catatonic at times. The deterioration of his motor function has been dramatic and all his medications need to be re-assessed.

Our girls stand beside me as their father is hospitalised. Sally comes with me on the morning of admission and I clutch at her desperately as the paperwork is completed and Steve is settled in the ward. Katie comes to visit her father later that day and sits curled up in a chair in the corner of the room, her back to her father, silent.

The drug, Cabaser, thought to have caused the psychosis, is removed, and the levodopa medication, Sinemet, is increased. It is not an easy transition. The delusions continue and the burly yellow-shirted security men frequently escort him back to the ward after his attempts to escape. He phones his elderly mother and friends and tells them the doctors are in on a conspiracy against him. He hides his medications. He calls his sister to keep a check on me. But after ten days, he is released. He isn't better but they send him home.

When Steve's psychosis is at its peak, I am despondent. His condition is so frightening and alienating that I can hardly associate him with the husband I have lived with so intimately for over twenty years. I don't know how to deal with his delusional state but Sally pleads with me, 'Don't give up on him, Mum.'

*

The psychotic episode, just three years after diagnosis, forces us to confront Steve's illness and to tell his employer of his condition. Steve is working in a non-government secondary school and initial reactions to the news are encouraging; his colleagues rally around him and the hierarchy seems supportive.

Steve slowly recovers from the psychosis but he needs to prove his ability to continue working and doctor's certificates have to be provided. After three months he resumes work part-time, and after another month, full-time.

Life becomes more positive. We enter a halcyon period where Steve's Parkinson's is well controlled with medication. His mental and physical state improves. We even travel to New Zealand on a family holiday.

*

April 2005. A cold night in New Zealand. The flight lands at Christchurch Airport at eleven p.m. We catch a taxi to the motel and unload our luggage. It is too early to go to bed – it is still only nine-thirty p.m. Australian time – and we are suddenly famished. I look out of the motel window and see a 7-Eleven across the road, still open, lights blazing.

We don our coats and head outside. It is starting to rain but we don't care. We hold hands and run giggling across four lanes, dodging cars, towards the store. I feel the rain on my face and the wind in my hair and I am ridiculously happy.

*

The euphoria only lasts for nine months. Towards the end of the year, new symptoms start appearing. Steve suffers excruciating foot cramps that cripple him. He endures profuse sweating and frightening panic attacks. The benefits of the medication last for shorter periods and he requires more drugs more often. His particular type of Parkinson's appears to be progressing rapidly. Although he tries to hide his symptoms, it becomes more obvious that he is struggling.

*

December 2005. Steve loses his job. He is called into the principal's office and told there is no position available for him the following year. There is no opportunity to work part-time. After twenty-seven years of service (twenty-two of them in the same school), his position is terminated.

We think about fighting this action. Isn't it discriminatory losing a job because of a disability? Isn't the employer supposed to provide suitable conditions for the employee to continue working, to help him in the workplace? We are told that the basis for his redundancy is not attributed to his illness but is due to numbers dropping in the school. If he contests the decision, he could be asked to prove his fitness to continue working. His employer would also withdraw the offer of supplementing his sick leave with additional benefits.

I am overwhelmed by the injustice of it all and overpowering feelings of self-pity emerge. Why did Steve have to get sick? Why is his disease progressing so rapidly? Why did he have to lose his job?

The demands placed on me as Steve's caregiver are also increasing. I book his doctor's appointments, buy his medications, run the home and manage our financial affairs. As he becomes more dependent, I need to help him on a more personal level. My attempts to care for him are based on my needs as much as his. I feel guilty that I am well when he is not. It is my duty and responsibility to look after him. But on a deeper level (and one I hardly dare acknowledge), I blame him for becoming ill, for disrupting the lifestyle we had once enjoyed.

After Steve retires from work, we are advised that he is eligible for government assistance. I have never entered a Centrelink office before submitting Steve's claim for the Disability Support Pension (DSP). When I arrive, the queue is so long it reaches the front door. I look around hoping no one sees me go in. I have a preconceived idea about welfare recipients – that they are all lazy 'dole bludgers' or single mothers with numerous children in tow, benefiting from the taxpayer's hard-earned money. I don't want to be dependent on the government for support; it goes against my beliefs and values. I resent filling out the forms that demand to know our personal, financial and medical details. I also don't want Steve to carry the stigma of being 'disabled'.

Despite the severity of his symptoms and the dramatic fluctuations in his condition throughout the day, Steve is rejected for the DSP. Centrelink is not convinced that Parkinson's is affecting his capacity to work:

> A decision has been made that you are not eligible for DSP because you are able to work thirty or more hours per week within the next two years. In making this decision, we took into account your skills, qualifications, work history and the medical evidence you and your doctor gave us. You may, however, be eligible to receive the Newstart Allowance or a Low Income Health Care Card.

It seems incredible that Steve has been refused but when we speak to an advisor at Centrelink, she tells us that the doctor has not provided enough detail in his report and that Parkinson's is a grey area because the rate of progression and presence of symptoms vary so widely between patients. 'Saying that Steve has Parkinson's is not enough,' she says. 'You're dealing with a government body now.'

After a more comprehensive evaluation from Steve's neurologist and an interview with a job capacity assessor at Centrelink, he is finally granted the DSP. Despite my earlier misgivings about entering the welfare system, I now understand that some people require assistance from the government and that our need is also justified.

*

April 2006. Steve's condition worsens and it soon becomes clear that to continue working would have been impossible. By now, he is on huge doses of medication just to get through each day. The neurologist asks whether Steve would consider surgery to treat his Parkinson's. Steve is keen – anything to alleviate the distressing and debilitating symptoms. He is referred to a medical team in Sydney for deep brain stimulation (DBS) surgery. Steve is assessed as a suitable candidate and a date is booked for November 2006. I begin counting down the days.

A small dose of Cabaser, the drug that had caused his previous psychosis, is reintroduced to help his physical condition until the surgery can be performed. I am uneasy and watch him carefully for signs of paranoia. He wakes one night and rushes down the hallway thinking he needs to get ready for school. I convince him to go back to bed but I lie awake for the rest of the night worrying the doctors will refuse to operate if he is displaying signs of confusion. They reassure me that Steve needs the surgery more than ever to enable him to reduce the troublesome medications.

Interrupted sleep and concerns over Steve's health are unrelenting. A friend offers to stay with him one night a week to give me a break from the nightly rituals. He sleeps on the floor in Steve's bedroom, getting up to help him to the toilet and to give him his medications. I pack an overnight bag and stay at our friend's house. I sleep for ten hours straight – deep, unbroken rest.

*

July 2006. One a.m. The medication he took at bedtime has worn off. He lies rigidly in the bed unable to roll over. I get out of bed and help him into an upright position. He sits on the edge of the bed.

I hand him his tablets and a glass of water. A string of saliva slowly escapes from his mouth and dribbles down the front of his top. He can barely raise his arm to swallow the pills. When he finally gets the tablets into his mouth, he coughs and almost chokes because the muscles in his throat are weak.

He needs to go to the toilet now, but when he stands, his feet are frozen to the floor. After some minutes, he slowly starts to shuffle forward but can't make the distance to the bathroom. I help him back to the bed. His need is urgent now. I quickly pass him the bottle but relief is slow in coming.

He wants to lie down but can't get under the sheets by himself. He is a big man and heavy to move. The best method is to push him over onto his side and then straighten his legs. I manoeuvre his hips back and his shoulder forward, then place one leg on top of the other. I pull the sheet and blanket up to his chin. The quilt is too heavy and he can't move under its weight.

Three a.m. He wakes drenched with perspiration. He can't regulate his body temperature and pools of sweat stain the sheets. By five a.m., he feels the familiar agony of nightly foot cramps. His toes curl under like claws, contorting his feet into impossible positions. The only relief he will get is from more medication.

Six a.m. At last, time for the next dose of tablets. He lies in bed waiting for them to take effect. After almost an hour, he is 'on' and able to get up and move freely. Right on cue the dyskinesia begins. His legs twitch incessantly, constantly on the move. But it is a small price to pay because now his Parkinson's symptoms have disappeared and he is able to function normally. He has breakfast, showers and dresses, all tasks that would be impossible without the drugs on board.

The respite doesn't last long. As the medication wears off, his Parkinson's symptoms return. He becomes increasingly anxious, his chest tightens and he feels as though he can't breathe. Sometimes he begs me to ring the ambulance because he is convinced he is having a heart attack.

I use an autoinjector to deliver a dose of apomorphine, a fast acting 'rescue' drug that will give him relief in under ten minutes. His body relaxes. The injection will keep him mobile until his next lot of medication. He is allowed five injections per day.

*

September 2006. Heavy sheets of rain pound the tall windows. Wide bands of water cross the pavement, the wind and rain drenching everything in its path. It is cold too, for September, and people arrive with coats over their finery, shaking umbrellas and adjusting dampened hairstyles as they enter through the heavy doors.

It is warmer inside despite the concrete floors and brick walls of this heritage building. The room is spacious with pendulous lights suspended from beams that support the high roof. Fairy lights are strung across vast expanses, twinkling in the nether regions of the hall. It is normally a large empty shell, just bare bones, but tonight the cavity is filled with large tables set for dinner. The flickering lights of candles dance across the crisp white linen tablecloths and catch the glittering sparkles that are strewn there.

The atmosphere is electric. Three hundred and forty-seven people have gathered here for a fundraiser to raise money for Steve's upcoming brain surgery. Friends and family unite in their love for Steve, donating their time and money in generous amounts. The gifts and prizes for the games and raffles have all come from various businesses, the result of vigorous campaigning by members of the fundraising committee. Several highly prized articles are being auctioned, a football jersey raising thousands of dollars. A well-known local celebrity offers his services as emcee. The entertainment is donated by artists eager to share their talents for a good cause.

We are unaccustomed to being the centre of attention, of being uplifted by the camaraderie of colleagues, family and friends. A constant stream of people comes up to Steve, offering love and support. Ex-pupils, some now in their thirties, reminisce with him about school days. They come to me too, and tell me, 'Mr Boulton was my favourite teacher!' Many express their admiration for him and the way they were inspired by him. The comments are spontaneous and heartfelt, a demonstration of affection and respect that is both humbling and overwhelming. I see Steve wipe his eyes. He is thrilled to see everyone and be supported by their love and concern, but he sees the sympathy, fear and grief reflected in their eyes. He observes their anguish as they bear witness to his.

The night is over all too soon. Like Cinderella after the ball, we are transported home at midnight, our chariot, a hire car provided for the occasion. We are euphoric, exhilarated by the night's events. But when we arrive home, reality sets in. Steve's medications have worn off and he becomes rigid. I help him prepare for bed and he sleeps a sleep of total exhaustion, but I am awake for hours, reliving the excitement, wanting the magic to last, reluctant to let the day end.

*

13 November 2006. The nurse turns on the light as she enters the room. 'It's time to get you ready,' she croons in her lilting Irish voice.

Steve opens his eyes but doesn't move. It is five a.m. and he's had no oral medication since midnight. An injection of apomorphine at three a.m. has worn off and now the full impact of his illness is apparent. I sit up on the stretcher bed beside him. I've lain awake all night getting up sporadically to help him roll over or use the toilet. I dress quickly, stuffing my blue satin pyjamas into a plastic bag.

I watch the nurse who, gently but efficiently, helps Steve into a shower chair and into the bathroom. The nurse laughs when she sees his night attire. He is wearing Superman boxer shorts.

'You'll be Superman after this operation,' she says encouragingly.

I share her laughter but Steve is silent. He sits rigidly, barely able to fulfil her requests but soon the hot water is running and the pre-op soap is lathered onto his skin.

The nurse works methodically, making sure any trace of sweat is removed. 'We don't want to risk an infection,' she tells him.

He longs for her to hurry up, for this ordeal to be over. She dries him and drapes towels around him to keep him warm, but even so he shakes. I murmur soothing words in his ear while the nurse bustles over to the bed. She strips the sodden sheets and remakes the bed with crisp white linen. The sheets have a strong hospital odour but Steve doesn't notice. His sense of smell has disappeared in recent years.

The nurse puts the compression stockings on him when he is lying back in the bed. His eyes are closed but soon his face distorts with pain. His feet begin cramping, the toes clawing and curling into grotesque positions. I move quickly to the bottom of the bed and start bending his toes back into their normal position. But as soon as I uncurl them, they start contracting again. Steve moans quietly, powerless to alleviate the agony. The nurse gives him two sleeping pills and the sedative quickly takes effect.

At seven a.m., the orderly arrives to take Steve to theatre. Our daughters have arrived just in time to see their father. We walk behind the bed as it is pushed down corridors and into the service lift. Tears roll, unchecked, down my cheeks. The stainless steel walls of the elevator, so cold and clinical, close in around me. They reflect a world of hospitals, doctors, and sickness, once alien, but now familiar.

Through more swinging doors and we arrive at the waiting bay. The anaesthetist speaks to us briefly. In the background, similar conversations are occurring as other patients wait for surgery. The curtains between the patients provide only a minimum of privacy but we are oblivious to others, our small family cocooned together.

*

I had arrived at North Shore Private Hospital the previous day. Steve had already been in hospital for three days in preparation for the DBS surgery while I'd stayed at home in Newcastle as Katie completed her Higher School Certificate.

Steve had been restless in my absence and his behaviour raised concerns. One day, he'd set out for a long walk away from hospital grounds and was gone for several hours. The doctor had admonished him but Steve had shrugged and joked about it. When he told me he could see large cockroaches climbing the dark brick wall of the building across the road, I became alarmed. He was clearly hallucinating and I was worried the operation wouldn't go ahead if he was mentally unfit.

I mentioned Steve's strange behaviour to a nurse.

She seemed unperturbed. 'Oh, patients often become a bit disoriented in the hospital environment,' she reassured me.

When the doctor visited on his evening round, we discussed the planned surgery. For the first part of the operation, Steve would be sedated but awake so he would be able to respond to the doctors. His head would be clamped into a vice so that MRIs and recordings of brain cell activity would enable the neurosurgeon to accurately position the leads and electrodes deep into his brain. The second part of the operation would involve inserting a battery pack and pulse generator, similar to a pacemaker, into his chest under general anaesthetic. The doctor warned us about the risks involved – the chance of infection or stroke.

I told the doctor about the hallucinations and about my fear that the surgery might have to be cancelled. He listened carefully, a concerned look crossing his face. He said he could still operate but that Steve's recovery might take longer than usual. He warned us that paranoia is a common post-surgery side effect and Steve's current symptoms might make this worse.

Steve was understandably nervous about the operation and the doctor told me that I could stay with him overnight. I hurried down the unfamiliar Sydney streets to collect some toiletries and nightwear from a relative's flat. By the time I returned, visiting hours were over and the security guard accompanied me to the third floor. I pushed open the double swing doors into the neurology unit and headed towards room 307.

*

Steve is in surgery all day. We visit him at four p.m., anxious to see him after a long day waiting. His head is swathed in bandages and he is sleeping. We leave the hospital, relieved the operation has gone well.

That night, the phone rings at two a.m. and I am startled from a deep, dreamless sleep. A nurse from the hospital asks if I can come and help settle Steve. He is awake and agitated and is asking for me. I dress quickly and drive to the hospital. The streets are deserted, the hospital car park empty. I am ushered into intensive care, where Steve is spending the night. He soon calms down when I speak to him and drifts off to sleep while I sit curled up in the visitor's chair, wide awake for the rest of the night.

The doctor arrives early the next morning. He rolls up his shirt sleeves and wakes Steve. He is hard to rouse at first, still sleepy from the anaesthetic. Then he is up on his feet, walking. The doctor leads him round and round the intensive care unit. He is happy with Steve's response to the surgery. He looks me in the eye and says confidently, 'When the walking goes well, it's a positive sign. It never goes backwards from here.'

*

Steve enjoys a honeymoon period following his surgery. In the first ten days, the positive effects of the operation are clear and his progress is remarkable. His mobility improves and he needs less medication. He has no 'off' periods. This heightened improvement is due in part to some post-operative swelling in the brain. As this subsides, he once again returns to having some fluctuations in his condition although he still needs far less medication to control his symptoms. The debilitating foot cramps disappear. He is able to get in and out of bed on his own and roll over in bed without assistance. He no longer has any 'frozen' periods.

Still, he expects more. He feels the operation hasn't helped enough. He wants the impossible – a return to normal. Medications are gradually increased and he has hospitalisations to tweak the settings of his brain stimulators until the optimum levels are reached. The doctors can do no more. We learn that Steve suffers from an emotional as well as a physical 'on' and 'off' with his Parkinson's. The medications cause an unnatural high. He becomes too happy, too energetic, too driven. Then the pills wear off and he becomes flat, unmotivated, depressed.

I slowly adjust to my husband's mood swings.

*

December 2007. We acquire Archie on Christmas Eve. It was never my intention to buy a dog – I didn't even particularly like dogs. We already owned a beautiful three-quarter Persian cat, Bella. I'd grown up with a menagerie of cats starting with the matriarch, a mottled black, white and ginger stray us kids had named Pimple.

We did have a dog once but he lives on the edge of my memory. Do I remember him or is it a photo I recall of a black bitzer with one blue eye and one brown? His name was Pluto and he tagged along with my older brothers as they roamed the bush behind our house. It was the late 1950s and I was barely five when he disappeared. The boys went looking for him, scouring the bush and eventually finding him under the lantana where he'd crawled to die. There was a tick buried deep into his fur but my brothers lifted him up and carried him home. Mum and Dad didn't take him to the vet. Maybe they couldn't afford it, but I just think it never occurred to them. They hardly ever took themselves or us kids to the doctor either. A decision was made to feed Pluto raw eggs and slowly he recovered, the home remedy gradually replenishing his strength. He survived the tick bite but vanished again later. Rumour had it that old man Perry who lived around the corner had a gun and a penchant for killing straying animals. No trace of Pluto was ever found and he disappeared from the pages of my childhood.

Katie sees the ad in the paper. She has just completed her first year of a veterinary science degree and thinks a cocker spaniel would be a good-sized dog for us. 'He'll be good for Dad,' she insists. 'You'll be able to take him for walks.'

I agree to look but remind her I'm not really interested in having a dog.

The puppy belongs to a breeder at Williamtown and we arrive at the rural property in the early afternoon. We follow the circular pebble drive to the front of the house and are met at the door by a woman in her late sixties. She wears a wide-brimmed hat and a friendly smile. Her face is weather-beaten, her hands gnarled. She tells us the puppy is eleven weeks old, the last of the litter. It is a warm afternoon and we stand under the shade of weeping willow trees while she goes through a high gate into a back yard hidden from view. She returns with a small bundle. His fur is black and silky and he has big brown eyes and long floppy ears. Katie takes him from the woman and he snuggles into her shoulder. Then Sally takes him in her arms. He has, despite his tender age, already perfected the soulful brown eyes and hangdog look. And he seems placid. I'm tempted. Perhaps it would be good for Steve to have a dog and he agrees to the purchase. It would give him an interest. Katie is right – we'd have to walk him, which would be good exercise for us both.

'If we get him, he has to be an outside dog,' I hear myself say. 'He's not to come inside – I don't want the house smelling doggy.'

The girls agree to all the rules I propose and soon I'm signing papers while the dog chews rocks at my feet. We put him in the car on the back seat between the two girls and drive home.

He sits quietly, his chin resting on his paw. We discuss names.

'What about Henry?' I say, thinking that he has a serious look. 'Or Archie?'

We discuss a few more options but by the time we turn into our driveway, it's settled. His name will be Archie. Steve, who has remained largely silent on the trip home, lifts the puppy out of the car. Later, I see him planting a kiss on Archie's head.

That first night, we make a bed for him in the laundry. We lay sheets of newspaper down, old towels and sheets for comfort, and close the sliding door. In the early hours of the morning, I hear him yelping and crying. Then he starts banging and scratching the door desperate to escape his prison. I lie awake listening to his cries wondering what I've let myself in for. The rest of the household sleeps undisturbed.

The following night, I leave him outside. He has the run of the backyard, but I'm worried that he might wriggle out under the side gate. I constantly peer out of the window checking to see if he's all right. We buy him a kennel and put it on the back veranda, where he can see us as we move around the house.

We adapt to Archie and he assumes top dog position. Bella is terrified and stays in the front yard or peers tentatively through the window at him. Archie barks and snaps whenever he catches a glimpse of her. I learn to peg the clothes on the washing line so he can't reach them – otherwise he destroys bras and eats undies. If he manages to get past us when we open the back door, he dashes around the house jumping on the furniture, scattering anything in his path. He devours used tissues and pees on the cream rug. He jumps on people. Puppy preschool and dog training prove fruitless. He escapes from the backyard several times and we chase him up the street. He'll settle down when he's been desexed, well-wishers tell me.

On the day of his operation, we pick him up and he wags his tail happily, pleased to see us.

'Keep him quiet,' the vet advises. 'Don't let him do anything too energetic.'

We go out for dinner that evening and leave Archie lying on his bed still sleepy from the anaesthetic. When we return home at eight o'clock, we find him gnawing an old bone recently dug up from the garden.

Katie goes back to uni in Sydney. Sally is busy with full-time work. Steve isn't well enough to help me. He shows little interest in activities and I am forced to take over most of the household duties. I'm also left looking after the dog and I'm resentful. When I confront the family, I'm met with silence; my rant is pointless. I consider returning Archie to the breeder. I'm angry that I was pressured into buying the dog. He's grown too big, too boisterous and is too much work. But he's part of the family now. I can't turn him away.

One late afternoon, Steve and I take Archie for a walk. We've started walking up the hill from our home when I realise I've forgotten my sunglasses.

'You go on ahead,' I tell Steve. 'I'll catch up with you.'

Back outside again, I see that Steve and Archie are still standing where I left them. Archie's tail wags expectantly when he sees me and I have to smile. We resume our walk, a twenty-minute circuit we regularly complete. The last leg is a steep climb up an unforgiving hill but we are nearly home. As we near the top, Steve starts bending forward and then begins lurching from side to side and I know he is about to collapse. I manage to steer him onto the grass before he falls to the ground. As my arms reach out to help him, I forget the dog and drop his lead. My mind is racing and I panic. I'm frightened Steve is having a stroke. The street is deserted and no one sees us. While I bend over Steve, Archie runs back and forth, occasionally sniffing and nudging him with his cold wet nose. Then he sits and waits dutifully as I attend to the patient.

After a few minutes, I help Steve to his feet. He hasn't hit his head or lost consciousness. His legs are working now and he seems alert but I am still shaking. I grab his arm and steady him before we set off for home. Luckily, we don't have far to go. The three of us head off down the hill – husband, wife and a black dog with a wagging tail happily trotting along beside us.

*

March 2008. Steve's apathy and mood fluctuations continue. I have adapted to the changes in his demeanour but the neurologist must think there is a problem because he sends Steve to a neuropsychiatrist. Steve goes unwillingly; he has always hated shrinks. The doctor is a short, softly spoken, kind man. I like him immediately but Steve doesn't. The doctor orders a memory test.

Steve fails the test. The doctor is tactful, subtle even. He tells us there is some memory impairment and that Steve might find it hard to acquire new skills.

Steve becomes angry and leaves the room. 'I'm not sitting here having you tell me I'm losing my memory,' he fumes.

The doctor leaves me on my own to digest this latest news.

Why have I not noticed a problem? I remember the barely cooked potatoes he'd tried to mash for dinner and his inability to work the microwave oven. I remember the way he couldn't replace the washer on the tap, a job he would once have easily completed. I think about his difficulty finding the right words and his sentences becoming harder to understand, crazy sentences we both laugh about. But I don't find anything sinister in the doctor's words. We know other Parkinson's patients who complain about forgetfulness – it's no big deal.

We drive home from the doctor's appointment in silence.

*

October 2008. It is almost two years since surgery. The doctor palpates the fluid-filled lump on Steve's head. It is a blister that has risen on his scalp and everyone is worried. The lump sits right on the wires in his head, a worrying sign that suggests an infection. We are in Sydney at North Shore Private Hospital and the neurosurgeon, neurologist and now the microbiologist have all had a look.

The neurologist is optimistic and tells us that if an infection is present, it will be treated with long-term antibiotics. However, the microbiologist warns us that an infection in the wires can't be successfully treated. Once an infection gets into the hardware, the only solution is to remove the wires and leads to prevent the infection travelling down into the brain. This is the worst-case scenario and my mind automatically shuts out this terrible outcome.

The microbiologist withdraws a minute amount of fluid from the blister and sends it to pathology. Steve is put on intravenous antibiotics as a precaution. The test results come back clear and I am reassured. It's not an infection after all. The doctor tells us he will see Steve in a follow-up consultation in two weeks. I pray the spot will miraculously disappear.

*

The neurosurgeon sits behind his desk and drums his fingers on its polished surface. He has palpated the spot again. It remains unchanged but there is high risk that the skin may break down. The doctor is undecided. He has rung his colleagues. Should he operate to remove the lump or leave Steve on life-long antibiotics to protect the wires? I stare out of the window at the panoramic view of the Sydney CBD.

The doctor makes his decision. He will remove the lump and clean the wires and surrounding area. The operation carries a risk of infection but if the blister bursts and the wires are exposed, the risk is even higher.

The surgery goes well. The doctor finds an infected suture, perhaps from the original brain surgery, although it seems unlikely the infection has been festering for two years. This time, the pathology results reveal the culprit – a normally innocuous bug that sits on the scalp. A PICC line is inserted into Steve's chest to deliver strong antibiotics and he is sent home a week later. I am given instructions on how to administer the medication through the line. A further course of oral antibiotics will finish the treatment. On our last visit to the neurosurgeon, the spot is gone and the scar is healing well.

*

December 2008. We have a holiday booked to Perth in early December. I deliberately avoid checking Steve's head before we go. I'm frightened of what I might see and I don't want anything to interfere with the trip.

Our next doctor's appointment is in Sydney on 16 December, a few days after we arrive back from Perth. The neurosurgeon takes Steve over to the window to have a good look at his head. As he parts the hair, we both see it. A new spot has appeared. It is filled with pus and I am filled with fear. This new spot is smaller but angrier than the first. We are told to contact the doctor immediately if any pus comes out. The doctor warns us that surgery to remove the deep brain stimulators is the likely outcome now. After a two-month period, and when they are sure the infection has healed, they will operate again to implant new wires.

On 23 December, after his morning shower, I see the pus oozing from Steve's head. With shaking hands, I ring the surgery. When I speak to the doctor, he tells me we have no choice now. The wires, leads and pacemaker will all have to be removed and he wants to operate the next day, Christmas Eve. I remind him that Steve is on a blood thinner. The high risk of a bleed in the brain means that the operation will have to be postponed until the blood thinner leaves his system.

Instead, Steve is admitted to North Shore Private Hospital for antibiotic treatment, by injection this time. I will need to administer the injections over the Christmas period. On Christmas Eve, with a nurse giving me instructions, I practise injecting an orange. Steve, as always, trusts me implicitly but I am nervous about this new responsibility. We go home armed with needles, antibiotics and orders to return the following week.

The doctors aren't happy when they check Steve's head six days later. The spot feels spongy and is still filled with pus. Steve is hospitalised in Sydney again and I drive back to Newcastle alone. It is my birthday. When my family ring, I sob into the phone.

Steve comes home on New Year's Day. Two days later, the skin breaks and I see the wires on his scalp. They look like thin metal worms crawling across his head. The operation needs to be performed as soon as possible now and surgery is scheduled for two days' time. The neurosurgeon returns from his annual holiday to operate.

*

January 2009. I arrive at the hospital early. Steve has showered and is bright despite having to face surgery again. Everything has been explained to us. The operation today will remove the wires and leads from Steve's brain and pacemaker from his chest. He will be in intensive care for twenty-four hours after surgery. A pump will be attached to his abdomen to deliver the apomorphine he'll now need. Without the benefit of the DBS, Steve's Parkinson's symptoms will be much worse. We expect to see a return to the rigidity, gait problems and foot cramping – crippling symptoms that tormented him in the past. The doctor expects Steve to be well enough to go home to Newcastle a few days later.

*

The operation is over. Steve is in intensive care, his head shaved, the incision on his scalp covered with a bandage. Katie cries when she sees him; it is a confronting sight and she is upset for her dad. The nurse tells us he is doing well, that all his vital signs are good. We speak to him and he answers with his eyes closed. He sounds like the old Steve and we feel reassured that he has come through this operation as well as can be expected.

In the following days, however, it becomes clear that Steve is not doing well. His Parkinson's symptoms worsen and he becomes rigid and uncomfortable. His neurologist is on leave and, despite my constant requests, the doctor looking after Steve does not visit until three days after surgery. By then, Steve is hopelessly under-medicated and we are both distressed.

One night, as I prepare for an overnight trip home to Newcastle, he lies trapped in the bed, incapable of moving. His eyes plead for help but I am powerless to comfort him. When the doctor finally appears, he says it is important not to over-medicate in the early days following surgery because of the risk of hallucinations and confusion. He sees that Steve is 'undercooked' and increases the dosage of his Parkinson's drugs.

Within days, Steve falls into a delirium. He sits in his chair looking at the ceiling, repetitively opening and closing his mouth. He can't hold a conversation or concentrate on the television. He suffers constant hallucinations and becomes agitated. He is prescribed antipsychotic drugs once again. The planned transfer back to the Newcastle hospital is delayed. Wards are closed because of the holidays and there is no bed available.

I am lucky I am staying with a relative in Sydney and do not have to commute back and forth from Newcastle. I spend long days at the hospital and soon I develop a routine. On the days I drive, I arrive at seven thirty a.m. to ensure a car park. Then I walk down to the oval and sit on a park bench until visiting hours start. I watch the personal trainers go through their paces with their clients, the early morning joggers, and the workers walking from the hospital car park to their offices on the highway. I go for long walks through the suburban streets breathing in the cool morning air before the heat of the day drives me indoors. Sometimes, I catch the bus to the hospital. It is only a twenty-minute trip and I am delivered to the hospital door. When I leave in the evening, I share the bus with strangers, commuters who are accustomed to the hustle and bustle of the peak-hour rush and the Sydney traffic. I am surrounded by people but I have never felt so alone.

Towards the end of January, I need to return to Newcastle for a minor surgery of my own. I am worried about leaving Steve but there is no guarantee when he can be transferred or whether his condition will improve. I finally decide it is better to have my own health issues addressed while he is being cared for in hospital. I leave Sydney in tears. I don't know how he will cope without my support and it will be some days before I can visit him. On the freeway driving home, a semi-trailer blasts his horn when I misjudge the distance between us. I pull off the road, shaking.

Steve is transferred back to Newcastle two days later. He doesn't arrive until eight p.m. after waiting for the ambulance all day. I later find out that he has missed several doses of medication and is rigid by the time he is admitted. The following morning, he is difficult to wake and seems unresponsive. Doctors and nurses come running and an EEG is ordered to see if he has suffered a seizure, but there is no sign of any seizure activity. I only find out this information when I arrive at the hospital at eleven a.m. When I speak to the doctor, I suggest that the symptoms were probably part of his Parkinson's 'off'. The doctor accepts my 'diagnosis' and acknowledges my close relationship as Steve's carer.

It takes several days before the timing of his medications is regulated and the nurses get to know my husband and I get to know them. I become familiar with the hospital routine and the various staff and patients on the ward. Every day, a cleaner wends his way down the corridor, pushing his bucket and mop. He sings as he works – Dean Martin, Frank Sinatra, Bing Crosby. His mellow voice serenades us all. I close my eyes and inhale the music.

*

February 2009. It is lunchtime when I arrive at the hospital. I am feeling guilty because this morning I had coffee with a friend and have arrived later than usual. I walk down the long corridors with the familiar feeling of dread. How will he be today? Will he be settled or agitated? What kind of night did he have? I am constantly struggling with mixed emotions. When I am with him, I don't want to leave because I know my presence calms him and I have some measure of control. When his medication is overdue, I can find a nurse to give him his pills. Don't they realise how important it is to have his medication on time? I can take him for long walks when his agitation is high, so that he doesn't have to spend all day cooped up in the ward. I sometimes see the relief on the nurses' faces when I arrive. The look says, 'Thank goodness, she's here,' and then I know he's been difficult.

At other times, I can't stand being in the hospital. I feel the walls close in on me. I hate the smells, the noises, the other patients. At one stage, Steve is in the stroke unit, where patients require intensive care. It's not because he's had a stroke. It's because the unit is closer to the nurses' desk and they can keep an eye on him. An elderly woman lies in the bed across from him. On the name board above her bed, someone has written 'Beautiful Betty' and I can see why. She is sweet and gentle.

One day, she looks across at me and says, 'Don't worry, love, he'll be all right.' Her words are comforting, her tone, motherly.

When Betty is moved to another room, I miss her.

I enter the ward today and head towards Steve's room. I find him sitting just inside the door of the room. He is strapped to the chair and is wearing a nappy. He is in full view of the passing public. I rush straight to him and bend down to his level. He whispers that he needs to use the toilet and I run back down the corridor looking for his nurse.

She tells me Steve was uncooperative this morning. 'He wouldn't have his blood pressure taken or have a shower,' she explains.

But I am furious and want to know why he has been restrained.

'Sometimes they settle down if you give them some quiet time,' she tells me, as though he is a three-year-old having a tantrum.

She bends down and unties the restraints and I can see that he is rigid in the chair.

'How long has he been sitting here?' I fume, and she tells me since eight o'clock.

It is now after midday. His lunch is sitting on the tray, untouched. I cannot bear to look at the nurse or speak to her, so I help Steve get dressed and take him to the toilet.

Later, Steve eats his lunch but I can't face food. I am sobbing quietly when a young blonde nurse who has looked after Steve comes to sit with me.

'That shouldn't have happened,' she says. 'This is a neurology ward and we expect patients to have these kinds of problems. We should be able to handle it.' Her concern is genuine. 'I just didn't want you to sit here crying on your own.'

Her kindness touches me but doesn't lessen my anger and grief over seeing Steve in such an undignified position.

I draw the curtain and we both climb onto the narrow hospital bed. We are cocooned there, hidden from the other patients. If I close my eyes, I can pretend we're not in a hospital, that Steve isn't sick, that I didn't witness his degradation. We lie side by side and I am weeping. The tears will not stop.

*

After several weeks with no improvement, the neuropsychiatrist suggests trying Steve on the drug Aricept, a medication used to treat Alzheimer's disease. The improvement in Steve's cognitive state is immediate. The first day he takes the tablet, he asks me how our dog, Archie, is and I know he is back in touch with reality. He becomes more like the old Steve, the one with a sense of humour, the one who is a loving husband and father.

The doctors in Sydney decide that an operation to replace the electrodes into his brain is now possible – indeed, it will provide the best chance for good quality of life for him.

'This will fix the mental health problems and get you back on track,' the neurosurgeon assures Steve.

The neurologist is more guarded. 'We don't know how well you will respond to the operation this time, given your current condition,' he warns.

Steve wavers, I waver. Should we go through with it again? The neurosurgeon puts the papers in front of us and Steve signs.

*

March 2009. The surgery goes well and the medical team is confident that they have re-implanted the leads in exactly the same spot as before.

Steve wakes up in intensive care and accuses me of being an imposter. 'You're not my wife,' he tells me. 'You just look like my wife.'

His voice, deep and gravelly from the anaesthetic, cuts through the beeping monitors straight to my heart. The doctor tells me not be concerned or offended, that this will pass.

A friend tells me this is my chance to hotfoot it out of there.

I bring Steve home two weeks later. The strange post-operative behaviour has settled, but something is clearly wrong. This is not the fun-loving man we all know so well. His personality seems to have undergone a major change. He is subdued and quiet. He can't stay awake past eight p.m. He is incontinent at night. His psychiatric medications cause constant drooling. His speech is confused. The psychotic symptoms persist. I am warned that Steve will be more reliant on me now, that he would not be able to manage without me. The doctors say it will take time for him to recover.

Instead, he deteriorates.

*

Night after night, I change wet sheets. Steve wakes every two to three hours and sometimes I am up three or four times a night. I often lie in bed sleepless, anticipating his call. The night-time incontinence is a new development that distresses us both. I begin trying various incontinence products, although it is a step neither of us wants to take. How I hate helping my husband into nappies. How embarrassed he must feel. But he doesn't resist. Eventually, we meet with an incontinence nurse who organises funding for the products.

Although Steve walks well, he becomes immobile when lying down. He can't roll over in bed and can no longer get out of bed on his own, so I buy him a bed stick to help him lever himself up. He refuses to use it at first, reluctant to become reliant on aids, but I insist. I am feeling the strain of helping this newly dependent husband.

Steve looks different. He has trouble closing his mouth and the drooling persists. He tries botox injections for this problem without success. The muscles in his face become more rigid.

One day, I catch him looking in the bathroom mirror. 'What are you doing?' I ask.

'Just seeing if I can still smile,' he tells me.

*

May 2009. Two months after the surgery, we go out for a friend's birthday. The restaurant is busy and Steve needs to use the bathroom. He is gone a long time and when he sidles into the seat beside me, he tells me that his pants are wet. The queue for the toilet was long and his need urgent. We are both mortified. We avoid social occasions for some time.

I'm working in an administrative role two days a week and leave Steve at home. I ring him regularly through the day, to remind him to take his tablets and to check up on him.

One day, I come home to find he hasn't showered or dressed. He can't tell me why he's done nothing all day. Why is he so apathetic?

In an effort to spark some interest and provide him with an activity, he joins a woodworking group. The doctor has told me to look for an interest with which Steve is familiar and, as a former industrial arts teacher, this seems suitable. I explain to the group that he has Parkinson's and ask if it is a problem. They assure me that they are happy to include Steve, but a few months later I'm called by the president. He has concerns about Steve coming to the group and is worried about his safety with the machinery. He tells me Steve doesn't participate. The voice on the phone is sympathetic but I am unaccountably offended. Steve does not return to the group. Instead, he joins the local gym, where the staff are kind and encouraging. The gym becomes a regular haunt and the young tanned girls behind the counter make a fuss of him.

*

July 2009. Steve has resumed the responsibility of looking after his own medication now and without my knowledge he stops taking the Aricept and the antipsychotic. I am upset when I find out and we argue. He refuses to take the drugs and becomes unusually agitated with me. We tell the specialist in Sydney about this omission when we visit him for a check-up. The doctor smiles. He is well aware of Steve's aversion to doctors and psychiatric medications. Although Steve's speech is still scrambled, there is no sign of psychosis and the doctor is encouraging. He wipes away any concerns, reminding me it will take time for the mental symptoms to subside after the recent trauma of the DBS removal and re-implant.

*

August 2009. I plan a holiday to the Sunshine Coast. Friends have offered the use of their holiday home and it seems too good an opportunity to miss. I pack extra linen, a rubber sheet for the bed, and the bed stick. We take two days to do the drive, staying overnight in a popular holiday spot. It is Steve's favourite destination on the coast, yet he seems uninterested. We sit on a bench overlooking the ocean eating ice creams, and I feel suddenly homesick and alone.

The drive through the busy stretch of the Gold Coast and Brisbane is stressful and I am in unfamiliar territory. Steve is no help as I navigate heavy traffic while trying to follow directions to our destination. We find the turn-off to Coolum but then I become hopelessly lost. It takes us hours, and several stops to ask for help, before we finally find the house.

Our stay is brief. Steve becomes confused in the house, unable to find his way around. When we go to Australia Zoo and the beautiful Sunshine Coast hinterland, he shows little interest. It is a lonely holiday and I miss the girls. I am worried too. What's wrong with Steve? Away from familiar surroundings, his condition is brought into sharp relief.

After a few days with little response or sign of enjoyment from Steve, I decide to drive home. We leave at eight thirty a.m. and I drive all day. After we have dinner at five p.m., I decide to keep driving. As the evening darkens into night, Steve starts hallucinating. The white posts along the road seem to bother him the most and I become alarmed.

We arrive home at nine-thirty p.m. after a thirteen-hour drive. I help Steve to bed then fall into bed myself.

He seems better the next morning. He doesn't say anything strange and I begin to relax. Perhaps it was just the change of scenery that confused him.

A week later, he wakes one morning and accuses me of having an affair with his friend. I persuade him to take the Aricept again and the delusions ease. I realise now that Steve will need to stay on this medication and my anxiety increases. I am frightened that Steve's cognitive problems may be permanent.

The following day, I call the neuropsychiatrist. When I press the doctor, he confirms my worst fear. He says Steve has a form of dementia related to his Parkinson's. He tells me not to worry, that Steve can live comfortably for many years with this condition, but I can hardly breathe. Wasn't Parkinson's enough? Now dementia too?

I am sitting outside in the warm spring sunshine, the phone pressed to my ear. The ornamental plum tree behind me is covered in pink blossoms. The scent of jasmine wafts through the air. I can hear bees buzzing. Steve is inside the house unaware of my call. I know that I cannot give him this latest prognosis.

*

December 2009. It is a typical Christmas Day – sunny, hot, the sky a brilliant blue. The cicadas are noisy this morning and I am transported back to Christmases in my childhood home.

My family lived on a two-and-a-quarter-acre block, with a white weatherboard house at the front and a large expanse of bush to the back. Every December, my father would search the bush behind our house for the perfect native Christmas tree. Sometimes, he would find a beautifully formed tree with evenly spaced branches; in other years, it would be lopsided, the branches uneven and drooping. My father would drag the tree back to the house and sink it into a bucket of sand while I opened boxes of decorations. Each bauble and trinket would be unwrapped from its tissue paper and a spot would be found on the spindly branches of the tree. Pine needles would fall to the floor as I worked, and a fragrant aroma would fill the room. When I was satisfied that the decorations were evenly spaced and the tinsel artistically applied, my father would place the star on top of the tree, a tradition that was upheld every year. Then we would step back and admire the spectacle. In later years, when my father was too old and frail to search the bush, an artificial tree was bought. It stood tall and symmetrical, each branch perfectly angled. Its shiny plastic leaves never moulted; it never leaned over on its stand; it never had that distinctive pine smell. And Christmas was never the same.

Now we are going to Sally's house for Christmas breakfast, the first in her new home. The Christmas tree stands in the corner and is bedecked with baubles and tinsel. A growing pile of presents is stacked under its branches. Sally's kitten, Oliver, jumps up at a decoration that dangles enticingly within his reach, and then leaps back, startled, when it drops to the floor and rolls under the table. We laugh at his antics, entertained by his skittish behavior and cuteness.

Soon, the table is laden with bacon, eggs, toast and croissants, orange juice and coffee. Steve sits at the head of the table because it is easier for him to get onto and off the chair from this position. He sits quietly and eats his bacon and eggs, a favourite, while our daughters and their boyfriends chatter happily. I am surrounded by loved ones but a familiar melancholy creeps in and once it starts, there's no stopping it. Nostalgia for my parents long gone, and for happier times when the children were young, washes over me. I sit quietly letting the emotions ebb and flow.

When the meal is finished, Sally begins handing out presents. Parcels are unwrapped, and gifts admired. The cat jumps in and out, under and over the growing pile of discarded wrapping paper. At first, no one notices that Steve hasn't opened any of his presents or that his face has crumpled and tears are tracking down his cheeks. The girls look on in consternation. Their partners, unsure of what is happening, sit in awkward silence. I help Steve up out of his chair and onto the back veranda, where sobs rack his body. I hear wailing and it takes me a moment to realise that this keening is coming from my husband.

'What's wrong?' I whisper, although I know the answer. I hug him tight and feel the despair in every muscle, the grief in every sob. I try to reassure him. Steve will be starting a new Parkinson's drug soon. 'Maybe the new medication will help,' I tell him.

'Nothing helps,' he moans.

And he is right. Nothing will help. While medications will provide relief from symptoms for short periods, the disease will continue on its relentless path and there is nothing we can do to stop it.

The wind picks up then, and the clouds scurry across a threatening sky. I stand with Steve as the world swirls and eddies around us.

*

February 2010. We are sitting in the doctor's clinic at the hospital. I have contacted the doctor previously without Steve knowing and have asked him to speak to Steve about his ability to drive. I have been worrying about his driving for some months, scared that he might have an accident and cause harm to himself or someone else. Although he is careful in traffic, he has trouble working out basic skills, such as putting the key in the ignition or turning on the windscreen wipers. Once, he reversed the car out of the drive and couldn't find the right gear to move forward. I have spoken to Steve about my fears but he ignores them. He loves his car and the freedom and independence it affords him and becomes annoyed when I raise the subject.

The doctor looks Steve in the eye and tells him that, due to his condition, he doesn't consider it safe or appropriate that he continue driving. The doctor reminds Steve that he suffers severe fluctuations in his health and that his medication does not always control his symptoms. He explains that he has the authority to stop Steve driving and will notify the RMS to inform them of his decision.

I am nervous about Steve's reaction. I feel as though I'm betraying him even though I know that for everyone's safety he needs to stop driving. I look across and see that his face has become white and pinched.

Then he stands up and says, 'I don't have to sit here and listen to this.' He storms out of the room, out of the hospital and starts walking home.

When I eventually pick him up, he doesn't mention the doctor's conversation.

In the following days, weeks and months, Steve forgets that he's not allowed to drive. When I remind him, he says he's perfectly capable of driving, that there's nothing wrong with him. He blames me for bringing up the subject with the doctor and is angry with me. His car sits in the garage, a permanent reminder of his loss, but he won't allow me to sell it. I hide his keys and he searches the house, room by room. I'm anxious to compensate for this latest deprivation, so I take him out constantly, visiting friends and going on picnics and day trips. It is exhausting but I know of no other way to lessen his pain.

One afternoon, his agitation is high and I cannot distract him. Now he wants to drive my car and demands my keys. I don't know what to do. Although I have managed to stop him driving his own car, a four-wheel drive, he has never shown any interest in driving my small sedan. I am worn down by the constant pressures and now feel bullied, so I drive to my brother's house, where I ring a helpline, desperate for advice.

The woman on the phone is unsympathetic. I explain the situation and am met by an uncomfortable silence. Perhaps she is making notes as I speak, because there are long pauses interspersing our dialogue. She asks me why I haven't sold Steve's car or hidden it from view, yet none of her solutions are practical or helpful. I find her attitude patronising and end the call. When I return home, Steve doesn't mention the car.

I remember when my elderly father lost his licence. He was already suffering from advanced Alzheimer's and the family had held its collective breath every time he took the car out on the road. My sister pointed out that he wouldn't be covered by insurance in the event of an accident but, even worse, we all worried our parents or innocent victims would get hurt. My brother, who once went for a drive with my parents, said that our mother would give directions as our father steered the car. With her own mental health deteriorating, she seemed unaware of the gravity of his condition. When he failed his compulsory driver's test at eighty-five, I told him not to worry, I would take him anywhere he needed to go. But the next day, he drove to the corner shop, the test and his loss of licence completely forgotten.

One morning, he rang to tell me the car wouldn't go. When I arrived at my parents' house, I found the car in the garage, the doors locked and the key in the ignition. I breathed a sigh of relief.

'You won't be able to drive the car,' I told my father. 'You can't get into the car.'

I looked into his clouded blue eyes and saw the confusion and distress. Once, he would have been able to work out a way to unlock the car door or would have known to ring road service for help. That sunny September day, just nine months before he died, he accepted my explanation and together we closed the garage door.

Eventually, Sally comes to collect Steve's car on the pretext that she needs it for work for a few weeks. He reluctantly agrees to this arrangement, believing it to be temporary. When Sally doesn't bring his car back, he thinks he can buy another. I keep distracting him but every time we pass a car yard his head turns and I know it's still on his mind. Sometimes, he insists I stop and he wanders around opening car doors as salesmen approach him. I can only guess the conversation that passes between them, because I watch from a distance determined not give him any support or encouragement.

Steve's obsession with his car continues, along with increasing hallucinations and delusional thoughts. He 'sees' car crashes and headless people walking along the footpath. One night, he tells me we have won money and need to go to the gym to collect it. When I ask him how he knows, he says our name was announced on TV. I always acknowledge these odd statements and never try to convince him otherwise, because, to him, they are very real.

The doctor, however, calls them 'strange thoughts' and quizzes Steve about their validity, antagonising him further. He prescribes an antipsychotic medication but Steve refuses to take it. Then, one night, I manage to slip a tablet into the night-time medication regime, unnoticed. Steve swallows the tablet with a gulp of water and the symptoms ease. As the months pass, however, he needs more and more of the medication to control his difficult behaviour and the dosage is increased. The addition of antipsychotics has an adverse effect on his motor function and his Parkinson's symptoms intensify. The rigidity and slowness of movement increase, the benefit of the Parkinson's drugs decreases, and his ability to function independently is compromised. The doctor tells us that Steve can be put on a different antipsychotic medication that is less likely to have these side effects. However, the drug is restricted and carries specific regulations. Steve will have to be hospitalised so that regular blood tests and monitoring can be implemented. The doctor begins the process for the hospitalisation.

*

May 2011. I take Steve to his parents' house, some twenty minutes from home, and we arrive at four p.m. It has been a difficult day, so I leave him with his parents and go shopping. I linger at the shopping centre, reluctant to go back and pick him up and am gone for just over an hour. I enter through the rear door and the house is quiet. I hear the muted sounds of the television coming from the lounge room. The house is small and it's soon clear that Steve isn't in the kitchen or living room, where his elderly mother usually sits. I start to panic. I don't even notice his mother, who is frail and ill and spends her days dozing in the chair. I move quickly to the main bedroom and find his father sitting on the edge of the bed.

'Where's Steve?' I ask urgently.

'I don't know,' he barks, and I run from the room, heart pounding.

Outside, the sky is darkening. It is five fifteen p.m. on a late autumn afternoon and I don't know where my husband is. He has no medications with him, no identification and he has decided to walk home. Which way would he have gone? Will I have to call the police if I can't find him? What if he tries to cross busy streets in peak-hour traffic? I reverse out of the drive and head in the direction of home. I choose the main road, although he may have walked down any combination of parallel or cross streets. I am driving slowly, eyes scanning each side street in the hope that I'll see him. A few minutes later, I glance to the right and locate him, on the hill, silhouetted against the setting sun. He is instantly recognisable, his stooped figure and measured walk the markers of his disease, now so familiar.

Relief floods over me but is soon replaced with anger. I am fuming when I finally pick him up. I stop the car in front of him and he smiles when he sees me.

'Why didn't you wait for me? Why did you start walking home? You haven't got any medication. How did you think I was going to find you? Did you think you could walk all the way home in the dark?'

The tirade continues even though I know it is futile chastising him. This impulsiveness is characteristic of his condition, and he thinks he is perfectly capable of the long walk home. Still, I become vitriolic as the pent-up frustration and fear bubble over and venomous words spew forth. It is a long drive home, him in bemused silence, me in tears.

A phone call a short while later brings the news that his mother has died. I take the call, but don't believe what I'm hearing.

'But we were just there an hour ago,' I stammer into the phone.

Now I must tell Steve his mum is gone. He seems to understand and we drive back to the family home to share this loss with his father and siblings. Death had come quickly. She had fallen asleep, forever, in her chair. I knew, then, that Steve must have been with his mother when she died, that it had happened in the moments before he left for the long walk home.

*

July 2011. Today, Steve tries to get dressed for the gym. He takes his jumper off. As he pulls it over his head, his T-shirt comes off too. It is a cold day and he stands bare-chested in the lounge room. There is a scar on each side of his chest reminding me of his two DBS surgeries. I see the shape of the pacemaker resting under his pale, freckled skin.

I suggest he put his shirt and jumper back on and he disappears to the bedroom. He returns wearing his T-shirt and jumper, but now he is standing in his underpants with one sock and shoe on, the other foot bare on the cold floorboards. His tracksuit pants are bunched up in his hand and he tosses them on the floor. He sits in the lounge chair and puts his other sock and shoe back on. I ask him whether he's going to put his pants on.

'Where are they?' he asks.

I point to the floor and he picks them up, still tangled, one leg the right way round, the other inside out. He fumbles for a few minutes trying to fix the wayward legs until I finally intervene. I kneel on the floor beside his chair and struggle to guide his foot through the narrow bottom of his trackpants leg. It's a tight squeeze because he has his joggers on. I repeat this procedure with the other foot and then help him into a standing position so that he can pull his pants up. The shorts he was originally going to wear are still in the bedroom and the whole procedure has taken some twenty minutes.

He is ready for the gym.

*

August 2011. Steve is admitted to Morisset Hospital. Morisset Mental Home. I flashback some fifty years to my childhood and stories of crazy patients thrown into the 'loony bin' spring to mind. Offbeat behaviour might be met with jokes about the place. 'Watch out or they'll lock you up at Morisset.'

I went to the Morisset Hospital grounds once when I was a child. It was for a picnic with my ballet group and I still have a black and white photo of that day. I remember the day and the photo because there is a little dark-haired boy in the group shot, maybe six or seven years old, the brother of one of my ballet friends. He is wearing shorts and a V-necked jumper and sports a short back and sides haircut. He's a skinny boy with knobbly knees and freckled skin. In the picture, he is eating an iced cupcake while his mother sits on the tartan picnic blanket beside him, talking to her friend. Just a few months later, he drowned in a drain in Cardiff, swept away while playing in the flooded canals that run through the suburb. The film in the camera was developed after he died and seeing him in the photo made the horror of his death even more real and present. How could he be gone? How frightened he must have been as those cold waters dragged him under. How desperate his mother must have been when he didn't come home. I clung to my own mother, scared of what could happen in a split second, when a child could be swept to his death, away from his mother and the living world.

Now I am entering the hospital grounds again, only this time it is with my husband. He is the patient, not some hypothetical loony. And this is not a joke. He is coming to the neuropsychiatry ward for treatment of his psychotic symptoms.

Morisset Hospital is considered when the private hospital system rejects him, claiming his needs are too high: 'We have an open ward here, it's not locked and we only have three nurses to twenty-six patients. Is your husband independent? He needs help with showering? He's incontinent? Confused? No, we can't manage him.'

So Morisset is the only option and I need to let go of the long-held stigma and fear attached to the place. Still, I feel my heart pounding as we drive in through the gates and begin the four-kilometre drive through bushland to the main entrance.

As we near the hospital, the bush gives way to open grassland where kangaroos lay sunning themselves, an unexpected carpet of furry brown bodies. This sight is so surprising we pause and take it in, marvelling at the spectacle. Now we pass buildings, old brick houses, some dilapidated with broken, barred windows, some functional. More buildings emerge as we slowly drive on and these, too, appear neglected, a relic from days past. When we turn the curve, we see a group of men approaching. They are a motley crew of four or five and they're accompanied by a minder. I am driving slowly in a wide arc to avoid them and I try not to stare. But as I pass, one man stands out, the leader of the pack. I notice that his tracksuit pants are too short, or is it because they are pulled up under his armpits? His T-shirt hangs off one shoulder. He has a basin haircut and his tongue lolls. He looks grey. Grey shirt, grey pants, grey skin. Institutionalised. I think of *One Flew Over the Cuckoo's Nest*. Then the minder, whose gaze has been averted, suddenly catches my eye and we are sharing the moment. I smile, then see his relief as he smiles back, and there is compassion and understanding between us – he with his charges and me with mine.

The hospital grounds are expansive and sweep down to the lake where the remains of an old fenced off swimming pool jut out of the water at odd angles. The sun beams down on the water and the ripples glitter like diamonds as they wash ashore. We follow a narrow winding road that traces the foreshore, before turning and driving up a gently sloping hill. A group of kangaroos hop across the road, some with joeys in their pouches, their heads poking out of their warm cocoons. An old man kangaroo with massive forearms stands grazing at the side of the road and looks up as we pass by, unperturbed by our intrusion into his territory. On our right, a church graces the hillside, its stained-glass windows shimmering in the light. It is neat, well maintained and clearly still operational because a sign on the wall says, 'Friday Service at 2 p.m.' It is an incongruous sight, this perfect church standing in isolation on hospital grounds where so many buildings have fallen into disrepair and decay.

Kaoriki House, where Steve will be staying, stands on the crest of the hill, a low, flat building with manicured lawns. The windows are covered with security grilles but at least they're not barred. A sign near the front door asks us to ring the bell – please press for one second and repeat if necessary – and a nurse jangling keys appears a few moments later. We are ushered into a wide hallway where a balding man ambles up, cricket magazine in hand.

'I'm Tony Lock,' he announces. 'I used to play professional cricket.' He flips through his magazine and adds, 'I'm fifty-two, I don't look it, do I?' He shuffles away oblivious to us, his surroundings, or the real world.

I hold Steve's hand tightly. What must he be thinking? I remind myself that the doctor has recommended this treatment and that Steve has agreed to try it. I utter a silent prayer. Please let him be safe here. Please let the medication work.

The doctor is not ready to see us yet, so we are led to an open area where a laminex table and chairs occupy centre stage. A kitchen bench and sink take up the length of one wall. On the opposite side are windows and a door that opens out onto a courtyard. The linoleum floor underfoot shows dirty patches, the sticky residue of spilled drinks and food crumbs. Long corridors veer off this main area leading to sparsely decorated bedrooms. Another door opens onto a lounge room, resplendent with plasma TV, lounge chairs, a piano and pool table. One wall has shelves that contain books, videos and games.

The nurse who shows us around apologises for the decor. 'It's old and basic,' she says, 'but the care's good.' She leaves us then and we are on our own.

Two patients look up from the pool table. One is tall and angular, the skin on his face pulled tight across his cheekbones. His hands are shaking. The other is shorter and covered in tattoos. We eye each other, the veterans and the novices. A woman sails by, muttering to herself. Her long hair is pulled back into a tight braid, her face expressionless. A young man, much younger than the rest, paces up and down the corridors, in and out of rooms, restless and troubled. He looks tired, his eyes are puffy and his tread is heavy. I wonder how such a slim young man can leave such a heavy footprint. I avoid eye contact, disturbed by his unsettled look. On the sofa sits an older man who yells out intermittently. Sometimes he laughs maniacally. He is slim and well dressed and has piercing blue eyes.

From outside, come the strains of Elvis Presley's 'Jailhouse Rock'.

The same balding man we met earlier comes to us, CDs and Elvis book in hand. 'Elvis was a great man wasn't he?' It is a statement, not a question, and he is standing very close. A string of saliva escapes from his mouth and dampens the front of his shirt and spots of spittle spray as he speaks. 'I'm Elvis. I'm a great man, aren't I?'

I nod in agreement, hoping he'll move on. I'm eager to escape his crazy babble but there is no way of avoiding the constant chatter. To my relief, the nurse comes back to announce that lunch is ready and we are led into a dining room where tables are set for the meal. The patients line up cafeteria-style for their food, which is served by a young woman wearing a pale green blouse, black pants and tightly fitting cap. There is something strangely discomforting about seeing Steve standing in the queue and I stand back against the wall, silent, observing this first step into institutional life.

After lunch, the occupational therapist shows us to Steve's bedroom. The room is bare except for a bed and cupboard. I unpack his clothes while the OT works out the best position for the bed. I warn her that Steve will need help rolling over and getting out of bed. I have a mental picture of him lying awake, unable to move, but she promises me that the night staff will check on him regularly. She hands me a couple of rubber-lined towelling pillow cases for when he comes home. Drooling is one of the side effects of this new medication. I shudder.

Finally, we are ushered into a small office where the heater is on and the room is too hot and stuffy. The doctor is at his desk and explains the treatment. Steve will start a new medication tomorrow to control the hallucinations and disordered thinking that have been troubling him. The protocol includes an increase in the medication every few days, daily observations of his temperature and blood pressure, and routine weekly blood tests that will continue when he leaves hospital. The doctor is casual and relaxed – we are on edge, uncertain, anxious.

Now, the moment I have been dreading – leaving. My heart starts racing in anticipation of the parting. I hold Steve in a tight embrace, my head resting on his chest. It is the same embrace we have shared for more than thirty years. It still holds comfort; it still reassures. Will he cope with this separation? Will I? We draw apart and I start walking down the endless corridor. The paintings on the walls blur as I hurry past. I turn once and see him, a lone figure, his arm raised in a silent wave. From the distance, I hear a voice calling out.

'I'm Jesus Christ. I'm going to save the world…'

Female Variation

When I was a little girl, my dream was to be a ballerina. I started dancing at six and loved it from the moment I donned my first pair of ballet slippers. My parents bought me ballet books for Christmas and birthdays and I would absorb every page. I loved looking at the photos of the ballerinas in their sequinned tutus and exquisite headdresses; my favourites were the English ballerinas from the Royal Ballet. Ballet pictures covered my bedroom walls. I even had curtains and a bedspread with ballet dancers on them.

Ballet filled a void in my lonely childhood. My parents were in their forties when I was born and my siblings had grown up and left home by the time I was eight. I was a sensitive child, filled with anxieties. My mother was loving and overprotective, and when the older children left, I became her focus. My father was stricter and had high expectations. I was to follow in the academic footsteps of my brothers and sister, who had all gone on to university. I attended a local primary school – just two classrooms and two teachers. It was easy to top my small class of ten students. As I reached the end of primary school, I started worrying about the transition to secondary schooling. But I was also relieved. There would be over a hundred students in my year at high school – surely now I wouldn't be expected to come first. When I achieved equal dux with another student in the first year, I knew that I would always have the pressure to perform.

Then my friend Judy died. Hodgkin's disease was brutal and brief. When I visited her in those final weeks, her frail thirteen-year-old body languishing in her parents' double bed, I knew she was dying. Her legs were as thin as broom handles, her skin alabaster white. She was worried about missing so much school, frightened she would have to repeat, but she never went back to school.

I worried about illness then. I worried my parents might die. I was frightened to be on my own. My father couldn't understand my fears and my mother smothered me, her own needs met by my dependence. Doctors and medications failed to ease my anxiety and eventually going to school was impossible. I was enrolled in correspondence schooling and so began a long, lonely period, isolated from my peers.

Ballet was my escape. It was a haven in which I could lose myself to the enjoyment of dance. Two or three times a week, I would attend class. At first, my fears accompanied me to the ballet studio, but soon the stretching and bending of my body and the joy of expression through movement and music proved to be the best medicine for my fragile mind. Slowly, I began to heal. After two years, I began dancing full-time and when I turned seventeen, I opened my own dance studio. There was never any doubt that ballet was my passion and that I wanted to dance.

Then I met Steve. He was laid-back and lots of fun and never worried about anything. He was a torment and a tease and, at first, I wouldn't know when to take him seriously. But gradually I became accustomed to his joking ways. He was always happy. And he shared my love of ballet.

*

My parents were Dutch immigrants. My father was born in 1909 and grew up in a small village in Friesland in The Netherlands. His father was a wiry little man, a baker, and his mother, a matronly housewife. Young Evert left home in his early teens, enrolled in a naval academy and became a ship's machinist. My mother, Tineke, was born in 1912 and grew up in the Dutch East Indies. The daughter of a wealthy bank manager and artist mother, she'd led a privileged life and travelled extensively. She met my father on a voyage home to Holland. Their shipboard romance flourished and they married on 29 August 1938.

They had settled in The Hague when war broke out. My father left the shipping line and was working but it was a time of deprivation and hardship. Food was rationed, the winters were cold and the German occupation of their country both frightened and angered my parents. Despite this, two children were born during the war and another two in the bleak years that followed. My parents rarely spoke about this time in their lives and photos of the period show a loving family with happy smiles. When the war ended, there was no work available for my father and by the late 1940s the decision was made to migrate to Australia.

In 1950, with four young children aged between eight and three, the family left The Netherlands forever. They boarded a plane that took five days to fly to Australia, with stopovers in different countries every night. The family first went to a hostel in Bathurst but were then relocated to Nelson Bay. My father found work and before long they'd bought a property and had a fifth child – me. My father was also able, with the help of an inheritance, to start his own toolmaking business – a lifelong dream. The old shed they'd been living in became his workshop, and the family moved into a new house built on the front of the two-and-a-quarter-acre block.

I have a photo taken of me on the veranda of our house. I am a blonde, blue-eyed five-year-old happily posing with a brightly checked parasol held over my shoulder. I'm wearing a pretty floral-patterned romper suit over a plain white T-shirt and thongs on my feet. I am pleasingly plump with a little pot belly, sturdy legs and chubby cheeks, and I'm smiling – a cute, cheeky grin for the camera. It's a sunny day and my eyes crinkle against the glare. Behind me, the distinctive white weatherboards of our new house gleam in the bright summer light. Later, when my aged parents become frail and ill and the family home falls into disrepair, I will remember these innocent days with nostalgia.

*

September 2011. Steve stays in Morisset Hospital for four weeks. The new antipsychotic, Clozapine, affects his Parkinson's symptoms. I notice a worsening on the first day of treatment; I can tell the moment I see him. He looks sluggish and slow. He has trouble chewing. As expected, he starts drooling. I ask questions and voice my concerns about the treatment. I am told Steve's body will adapt to the medication and the side effects will ease. The protocol continues as planned and he comes home on a hundred milligrams.

We now have a weekly appointment at the mental health clinic. The secretaries sit behind security glass and the nurse ushers us beyond a locked door to a small room where the doctor is waiting. He reminds us that this drug is usually used to treat schizophrenia. At this first meeting, he tells us that he knows nothing about its use for Parkinson's disease.

Steve sits quietly beside me. The medication is very sedating and he is so sleepy he can barely hold his head up. The doctor seems bemused by Steve's condition and long pauses punctuate our conversation. Finally, he suggests lowering the dosage to seventy-five milligrams. I am surprised by the doctor's indifference and walk out of the clinic angry and disheartened.

When Steve starts lurching, his body bent double, I contact the neuropsychiatrist. He reduces the dosage again to fifty milligrams. When Steve shows signs of seizure activity, the dosage is reduced to twenty-five milligrams.

The hallucinations continue.

*

October 2011. Steve lies on his side on the edge of the bed, his knees pulled up to his chest. I bend over him, a suppository clutched in my gloved hand. The combination of Parkinson's disease and his various medications has caused chronic constipation and Steve is now suffering from overflow diarrhoea, a symptom of bowel impaction. When copious doses of laxatives fail to shift the blockage, I finally try the suppository. I'm nervous and embarrassed about the procedure but Steve waits obediently, trusting me. Several hours later, it is apparent the suppository has failed.

At our next visit to the mental health clinic, I mention Steve's ongoing bowel problem. I tell the doctor about the laxatives, the failed suppository and my distress.

The doctor laughs at me and shakes his head. 'You give up too easily,' he tells me.

When I burst into tears of rage and frustration, he leans back in his chair, his fingertips pressed together in a prayer-like position while I sob and rant uncontrollably. His silence infuriates me.

The bowel impaction is eventually cured with heavy-duty purgatives and a visit to casualty at the local hospital. With Steve's intestines cleared, I must now ensure that the problem doesn't recur. I check his toileting habits daily and mix laxatives into his orange juice every morning. I increase the fibre in his diet.

Later, when eating is difficult and Steve's weight plummets, we are referred to a lovely young dietitian. She suggests protein and dairy-rich foods, and eventually, a dietary supplement to help with the weight loss and his intestinal health. 'Make every mouthful count,' she gently advises, so I add cheese, sauces, ice cream and daily milkshakes to his diet.

I become an expert on Steve's condition. I know his body better than my own. I recognise when he needs more medication and when he needs less. He ingests a heady cocktail of drugs daily. Sinemet for mobility, Clozapine for psychosis, Exelon for cognition, Citalopram for depression, Fortisip for nutrition, Osmolax for elimination. The medications are finely tuned, the balance between treating the physical and the psychiatric symptoms hard to get right. No two days are ever the same.

*

We are allocated a case manager who arranges some home help. She meets with us to discuss our needs and to broach the subject of a personal care assistant for Steve. The case manager is tactful and considerate and Steve agrees to a trial. I do not want strangers in my home, and feelings of betrayal and disloyalty surface, but I need help. Three mornings a week, an assistant will come to our home to give Steve a shower and shave.

The first day, I get out of bed early and tidy the house. I'm nervous and want to create a good impression. There's a knock on the door and I see a middle-aged woman with fair hair tied back in a tight ponytail. Her manner is short and unfriendly and I dislike her immediately. After the introductions, I show her to the bathroom. I leave Steve in her care and retreat to the kitchen to wait.

Steve emerges from the bathroom twenty minutes later showered, shaved and dressed. He looks clean and fresh and seems unperturbed by this new experience. The care assistant follows him into the kitchen and thoroughly washes her hands, as though contaminated, while I stand awkwardly in the background. I can tell that she is efficient and Steve later tells me that she is kind, but she seems cool and impersonal.

One morning, some months after the service has started, Steve becomes agitated and uncooperative. The assistant, her round face flushed, loses her composure and I am summoned to the bathroom, where Steve is standing half undressed. A scowl darkens his face.

'I'm just trying to help him,' the aide complains while I try to placate them both.

Steve looks me directly in the eye and asks sarcastically, 'How much are you paying her?'

*

November 2011. He is lying in bed. He can't sit up by himself, so I roll him onto his stomach and swing his legs off the bed. Now he is kneeling on the floor with his hands on the edge of the mattress. Slowly, he pushes himself up onto one foot, then the other. I help him up by lifting him under the armpit until finally he is perched on the edge of the bed.

His eyes are closed. It's not because he's asleep. He can't open them because the muscles around his eyes don't always function. A string of saliva spills from his mouth and wets his T-shirt. I give him tissues and he slowly dabs his mouth but more saliva escapes. It has been building through the night. Last night, he woke choking with spit. The sheets and pillowcase were saturated with slime.

I offer him a drink of water. I lift the glass to his lips and, if he is able to swallow the water, I give him his first pill for the day. Sometimes, it sits in his mouth and he can't get it down. When that happens, the saliva turns orange as the tablet starts dissolving in his mouth. Once he swallows the tablet, we work on getting his eyes open. I physically prise top from lower lid with my fingers and often this is enough to trigger their opening. Sometimes, standing up will also trigger the opening response. At other times, we just have to sit and wait until the medication has taken effect.

I help him to his feet. He is stooped, eyes fluttering between open and shut. He looks unsteady, so I hold his arm. When I suggest we start moving, his feet won't work. They are stuck to the floor though his body wants to move. Suddenly, he lurches forward, as though about to fall. Then he shuffles to the bedroom door, pausing at the threshold. I tell him to step forward and with a bigger stride he is through the doorway. We turn and I guide him down the hallway, my arm in his. The day has begun.

*

December 2011. Why does Steve's condition vary so much from day to day? The medications are the same, the routine is the same, and yet there are fluctuations in his demeanour, physical state and cognitive abilities.

Tonight, Steve is obsessed by a small fly that is buzzing around him. He tells me it's a big red spider and tries to swat at it with his hand. He is eating a bowl of ice cream, but even that doesn't distract him from the fly. It keeps annoying him, this tiny insect, as it lands on his leg or arm. We both watch it now. Several times, I come close to squashing it, but the fly senses my movements and darts away only to swoop again and again. I wait until it lands on Steve's foot and then hops onto the floor, a small dark spot on the polished floorboards. I pick up a shoe and inch forward, careful not to make any noise or sudden movements. I whack the shoe down quickly and kill the fly. Steve finishes his bowl of ice cream.

*

January 2012. We are out for dinner. It is a special celebration for Aaron, Sally's fiancé, on his birthday, and his extended family are joining us. I don't want to have dinner with strangers. I'm now embarrassed on social occasions, especially when we meet new people. I often try to cover for Steve so that his diminished capacities are less noticeable. Yet nothing can hide his stooped posture, open mouth and confused look.

Dinner is at a Mexican restaurant and we arrange to meet outside the entrance. I see a group of people already waiting and guess they must be Aaron's relatives. We wait some distance away until I see Sally and Aaron arrive. I wonder if Sally realises my discomfort or if she feels uncomfortable in this situation. But she smiles and hugs us, and we are ushered into the restaurant and seated at a long table. I ask if we can sit at the end of the table to make it easier for Steve to get up and out of his chair. That's not the only reason. Perhaps if we are at the end of the table, we will be less obvious. I'm always trying to orchestrate situations to make them easier for Steve and, lately, for me.

My discomfort increases when the meal is served. Steve's motor skills have deteriorated and I'm worried he won't be able to manage the meal. I fear he will cut off huge chunks and try to stuff them into his mouth, that the food will hang from his mouth as he tries to manoeuvre it in, and that he will be oblivious to there being a problem. So, without asking him, I pick up a knife and fork and cut his food for him. He allows me to do this. I do it as quickly as possible and do not look up from my task, although I am aware others are watching. He starts eating and I begin my own meal, watching him in case he needs help. This interference must annoy him, but he says nothing.

Later, Steve rests comfortably, exhausted from our evening out, but I lie in bed, sleepless.

*

I hate it when he's agitated. He becomes restless and starts pacing, wanting to go out. I don't recognise the look in his eye. Who is this man? I know he can't help it but it scares me. He's not physically aggressive, but there's a forceful quality that is unsettling. It's the demanding nature of his behaviour that frightens and upsets me.

*

February 2012. We are sitting at the dining table with Steve's dad. The table is covered with a green vinyl tablecloth and littered with letters, pens, jars of screws, lollies and other paraphernalia. At one end of the table is a 'placemat', a few layers of newspaper positioned to catch spilled food and drink. A tomato sauce bottle sits in front of the placemat, the sauce congealed around the spout. Next to the sauce bottle is a Coca Cola bottle filled with water. The old man eats his meals off old NSW Railway plates. They were pilfered years ago when a distant cousin worked for the railways and they have been in constant use ever since. They are small plates yellowed with time and marked with spidery lines. The red Railway emblem on the rim is faded but still visible. A good set of patterned china sits in the cupboard but has never been used.

The room is dimly lit, although it is only early afternoon. The blinds are rarely opened and the lights never turned on during the day. The walls are painted a pale grey and are peeling, and the carpet under the table is stained and worn. There is a photo on the wall of Col and Jean, arms linked, on their wedding day. She is wearing a pink dress and hat with her hair pinned into a popular 1940s hairdo, a style she wore for the rest of her life. He is handsome in his army uniform. They stand together smiling, a typical wartime bride and groom. Next to the photo is another frame containing two golden wedding anniversary cards. They are inscribed with words of love to one another on the celebration of fifty years of marriage.

The old man sits alone now. He is wearing an old pyjama top and cut-off shorts. They used to be tracksuit pants until he attacked them with a pair of scissors. His skinny legs are exposed from the thigh downwards and I see knobbly knees and discoloured calves in lurid shades of purple and blue. His ankles are swollen because he sits up all night in a chair and his circulation is poor. He has on thick woollen socks and slippers although the day is warm. I wish he would wear some of the nice clothes he owns. The shabby garments are depressing and the room cloying with the musty smells of food, disinfectant and old age.

The old man is eighty-seven and in better form than his son. He is alert and coherent, and relatively independent. Old age has made him hard of hearing, cantankerous, stubborn and demanding. He was always the head of the household, the strict patriarch who ruled the home. I was often wary of him when I was younger, unsure of his attitude to his wife and children. He never once raised his voice in anger to me, but the other family members were often verbally abused. Then, at the age of sixty, he suffered a massive heart attack and died in the ambulance on the way to hospital. He was revived and when he woke up said, 'Gee, that moon's a long way away.' Although he survived the heart attack, he never regained his strength and zest for life and spent many years suffering depression. Myriad other ailments also fed into his hypochondria but incredibly, and much to our mutual disbelief, he's still with us. It seems unfair that he can function so well at eighty-seven and his son is struggling so much at fifty-seven. But to focus on the injustices of Steve's condition is pointless, so I try to concentrate on what he can still do to have the best quality of life.

Now, his father looks at Steve in silence. He says nothing at first, just observes his son sitting on the chair. He sees the drooling, the confusion, hears the unintelligible speech. Then Steve stands and moves to the lounge room and I see him watching his son's stooped figure filling the doorway.

The old man looks at me, shakes his head and says, 'You've got your hands full, haven't you?'

I nod and then look away because this unexpected show of compassion catches me and the tears well up. We sit like that together in silence for several minutes until Steve re-enters the room and I am composed again. We rise to leave and the old man asks me if I'm all right, and I am, because this rare show of concern wraps a warm hand around my heart.

*

I am angry with Steve this morning. When urine escapes onto the bathroom floor, yet again, I become annoyed. Every morning, I get up to saturated incontinence pads and damp sheets, evidence of his failing body and mind. Today, he doesn't sit on the toilet properly and the urine trickles down the bowl and onto the floor, encasing his feet in a pool of yellow liquid. He stands up, unaware of what has happened and walks the foul fluid the length of the hallway, leaving damp footprints all the way. I berate him, pointlessly, and then I feel ashamed.

My first job for the day is getting a mop, bucket and disinfectant and cleaning the floors. Luckily, we no longer have carpet in the living areas. The bedroom carpet has a lingering odour despite professional cleaning and multiple applications of carpet deodorant. I am reminded of the aged care facility where my mother spent her last years. The smell of urine assaulted the visitor at the front door and pervaded every room. The nursing home was carpeted to create a quieter, more homely feel but the carpets harboured an unpleasant aroma.

Now my own house is under threat. I worry that the offensive smell will infiltrate every room. I clean the toilet daily, multiple times, and keep a mop and bucket handy. But the smell of disinfectant mingled with urine creates its own perfume and is just as invasive and unpleasant. Even the commercial air fresheners I purchase to mask the smell have their own nauseating effect.

*

I'm sad today. He seems to be getting worse. Sometimes, he can't sit up straight in the chair. He leans over sideways, his right cheek on the arm rest, the knuckles of his right hand brushing the floor, his big blue eyes staring. I try to raise him to an upright position and he groans as I straighten him up. Moments later, his body bends over again as limp as a rag doll.

He's barely talking. His speech, a tangle of unidentifiable syllables and words, defies meaning. I look for clues to unravel the mystery like a detective trying to solve a crime. When his sentences emerge clear and precise, I feel like cheering.

I don't know how to amuse him. He can't read any more or help me with simple household tasks, so I turn on the television to entertain him. He has always enjoyed watching TV but now it lulls him to sleep. He sits in his chair, chin on chest, blue eyes closed.

Tonight, I help him into bed – our nightly ritual. He gives me a little wave as I leave the room and I blink back tears. Sometimes, horribly, he's aware of what's happening to him.

*

March 2012. The anxiety is overwhelming. It envelops me like a shroud. It is paralysing. A small darkened spot sits on the wires in Steve's head. I've seen a similar spot before, a small innocent bruise on the scar line. It was checked and proved to be nothing. But I'm worried. Does this one look darker? More lumpy? What if it's another infection? Should I take him to the doctor or am I being paranoid? The indecision is torture.

The neurologist finally checks the spot but he has no answers. It doesn't look like an infection but there appears to be some trauma to the skin near the wires. The uncertainty of not knowing means that I will have to be vigilant. There is a constant nagging worry that it may develop into a serious problem.

*

The neurosurgeon in Sydney has had a look at the spot and it's not an infection. However, he thinks it may be the beginning of an 'erosion';

the wires are starting to break through the skin. He palpates the spot and comments on the skin being thin. He asks whether I've noticed any fluid seeping out and I shake my head. If the skin breaks and the wires are exposed, there is a high risk of infection. Alternatively, an operation to move the wires into a less problematic position also poses a risk of infection.

I see the surgeon mulling over the options. He takes photos of the spot, first on his mobile phone and then with a camera. We discuss the possible causes. It seems most likely that the skin has worn thin because Steve sleeps on that side of his head for ten or twelve hours every night. It is his most comfortable sleeping position. He cannot roll over in bed. To turn onto the other side he has to get out of bed and then get back in again. The doctor tells us he mustn't sleep on that side of his head any more. He says if the pressure is relieved, the skin will possibly recover, thus avoiding surgery. He tells us to make an appointment for six weeks' time, shakes our hands and we head back through the Sydney traffic and onto the freeway back to Newcastle.

*

Tinkle tinkle…tinkle tinkle…TINKLE TINKLE. The sound of the bell ringing becomes louder and louder, finally penetrating my sleep. I struggle to open my eyes. I have been dreaming, deep in an exhausted sleep, and I don't want to let the dream go. But the bell is insistent, the dream recedes, and I'm on my feet, staggering in the fog between sleep and wakefulness, down the hallway to Steve's bedroom. I have given him the bell to ring when he needs me. He can't call me because his voice is too weak when he's lying down and he can only manage a whisper. For the past six years, I have slept in a separate bedroom because he is restless at night, twitching constantly.

The disturbed sleep started years ago, before he was diagnosed, and is a common symptom of Parkinson's disease. It was one of the first symptoms that we noticed, although we didn't know it at the time. Acting out dreams is another frequent problem. One night, I woke to find

Steve crouched on all fours beside the bed. He had leapt out of bed, his teeth knocking the bedside table on the way, and landed on the floor. He said he'd dreamt he was a panther pouncing on his prey and we laughed about the bizarreness of it all. Then, another night, he threw a punch in his sleep, his fist connecting with my mouth. Some years later, when his Parkinson's was more advanced, I woke in the early hours of a summer morning to a loud crash. I ran to his room to find him on the floor beside the shattered floor-length window. He had a large bruise on his shin and some minor lacerations near his ear. The carpet and veranda outside the bedroom were littered with broken glass. He'd dreamt he was performing a karate move.

Sometimes, he calls out in his dreams. Often, his ravings consist of incoherent babble or maniacal laughter. At other times, his voice is crystal clear, loud and authoritative. I hear the schoolteacher in him resurfacing in his dreams and am surprised by the strength in his voice, because during the day he is quietly spoken and often quite hard to hear.

Now, I need to monitor Steve to make sure he stays off the spot on his head and have been camping on a mattress on the floor of his room. I am uncomfortable on the mattress, my bones pressing through the thin foam and digging into the floor. I sleep fitfully, rousing at every sound and movement he makes. If he gets out of bed, I have to make sure he gets back in on the right side, because he won't remember. Sometimes, sleep is impossible.

I take him back to the neurosurgeon after three weeks. The doctor is our age, tall, slim, good-looking, charming, vibrant, successful, self-assured. I can't help comparing his lifestyle to ours, his health to Steve's. I look at his hands as he examines Steve's head and see that his fingernails are very short. I wonder if he bites them, if underneath his confident exterior lurk insecurities.

After the examination, the doctor sits behind his polished desk and looks at us both. The spot is no better or worse but he sees my fatigue and distress and decides that an operation to move the wires will be necessary. If the skin breaks, the risk of infection is high so he would prefer to treat the problem in a controlled environment, but I feel as though I have failed, that I have been unable to protect Steve from this new problem. The doctor tells me to go home and sleep, that I can't stay awake for twenty-four hours a day keeping watch, that we are all in this together, and that I have done as much as I can.

Tonight, I am back in my room. The bed is deliciously soft after sleeping on the floor and I sink blissfully into the mattress. I know my sleep will be broken soon, that he'll ring the bell and need my help but I will try to make these night-time interruptions as brief as possible. And when he is settled, I will pad quietly back down the hallway, back to my lonely bed.

*

I wake up early on the day of Steve's operation. I'm nervous and apprehensive about the procedure but relieved that the skin on his head has stayed intact. I don't want him to go through more surgery but it is inevitable, this constant dance with treatment.

I want to get to the hospital early to make sure I see him before surgery. The operation is scheduled for early afternoon, but I arrive mid-morning. I find him freshly showered and in his surgical gown and stockings. He is in bed, and I think that is unusual because he never rests in bed, even at his sickest.

Our daughters are with us. I'm glad they've come to be with their dad today. I'm glad to have their company. Steve is patient. He dozes intermittently while we take it in turns reading the paper and watching TV. A nurse comes to tell us the operation has been delayed for a few hours. By now it is one p.m. and we are all hungry, so we leave Steve and head down to the hospital cafeteria. We are faced with long queues and it is noisy in this cavernous basement food hall. There are no vacant tables and, after standing in line for ten minutes, we decide to try the hospital café instead. Back outside and across to the private hospital, past the courtyard with its escapees hooked up to IV drips and cigarettes, past the nurses on their lunch breaks, past the doctors, stethoscopes around necks as they hurry between patients.

We walk in through the front doors of the hospital, although the entrance is more like a hotel lobby than a hospital reception area. The marble floors, columns and furniture are stylish, and people sit on elegant lounges reading newspapers. An elderly valet opens car doors for visitors and directs traffic through the narrow drop-off zone. He wears a suit and is immaculately groomed. I have to remind myself that this is a hospital and not a holiday destination, that sick people reside here, not hotel guests. I am reminded that this is Sydney's wealthy North Shore and I feel a long way from home.

The café is busy but we find an empty table. I stand in front of the refrigerated display cabinet and see a variety of sandwiches, rolls, Turkish breads, gourmet pies and sausage rolls. I don't feel like eating but settle on a ham and cheese toastie because it's the cheapest item there and I can't face anything more exotic. When it comes, it is surprisingly good and I discover that I'm suddenly ravenous. I bite into the sandwich and the cheese oozes out, creamy and smooth. I wolf it down and feel better, the warmth of the food filling my empty stomach. I become addicted to this simple meal and order it every day. Having lunch in the café reconnects me to the human race and provides a brief respite from the hospital room, the sick husband, the carer role.

Before long, I worry that I should go back to Steve's room. I'm frightened that they'll wheel him down to surgery before I get there. I want to be with him, to kiss him goodbye. I want to see him one last time before the anaesthetic, because I don't know what he'll be like after it. Will he be more confused when he wakes up? Will he know us? Will he be paranoid or psychotic? I am prepared for every eventuality. It is important that I see him one last time, just in case, so that I can imprint the way he is now onto my mind.

Of course, Steve is still in the room when we get back and we wait another two hours before they come to get him. The orderly wheels him into the elevator and down two levels to the surgical reception area.

A lovely young nurse bounces in and introduces herself as his anaesthesia nurse. She checks his details, explains the procedure and I sign consent forms. Even as I sign, I wonder if I am doing the right thing. But I don't really have a choice. The wires need repositioning or they risk pushing through the skin. Surgery seems to be the lesser of two evils.

'Look after him,' I tell the nurse, and she gives me a breezy smile as they disappear down the corridor and out of sight.

Eight p.m. Steve is wheeled into the room and suddenly there is a bustle of activity as the nurses cluster around. The wound on his head is oozing and the pad on the pillow is saturated with blood. This causes some concern and a phone call is made to the surgeon, who suggests a compression bandage to stem the flow. I stand back, because this is out of my hands and I must rely on the professionals to look after him. The nurses reassure me that the bleeding is contained and that his vital signs are good. But I see a damaged man, helpless on the bed.

He knows I'm there and holds my hand. He mumbles a few words and I know that he recognises me. Our daughters say goodbye to their father and leave for the two-hour drive home. I kiss him goodnight and take the elevator down to level 1. I walk down the long corridor, past intensive care, past the operating theatres to the front of the hospital, then take another elevator ride down to the ground floor. The foyer is empty now except for a security guard and receptionist behind the desk. My footsteps echo on the tiled floor. I pay the parking fee, and then it's another elevator ride up to the fifth level. My car is parked at the far end, the only vehicle there now, but the area is well lit and I'm not afraid. I walk slowly to my car, drinking in the fresh night air.

*

Steve recovers well from the surgery. The spot has been removed and the wires moved to a better position where they are less likely to cause friction. The neurosurgeon is pleased with the result and we travel home to Newcastle. When I help Steve into bed, I encourage him to stay off that side of his head.

*

April 2012. Steve looks out of the kitchen window and tells me he can see two cats playing golf.

*

Tomorrow, Katie is leaving home. She'll be sharing a house with her fiancé, Mat, and I should be happy for her. I am happy for her. But now there'll be no one to talk to in the long hours after Steve goes to bed. There'll be no one to distract me from the monotony of my day. There'll be no one to share the caring.

My two little girls have grown up and left home. I should be pleased they both did well at school and university and have grown into capable, independent women. I should be pleased they have both found partners who love them. I should be pleased not to have to do their washing, ironing and meals any more. I should be pleased the bathroom vanity stays clear of make-up, cleansers and moisturisers, and there are no hairs clogging up the plughole. I should be pleased that there are no unmade beds, no clothes strewn around the bedroom, no damp towels dropped on bedroom floors.

I remember when I became engaged. I was the last of five children to leave home and as my siblings had all moved away from Newcastle, some to other states, my parents relied heavily on me. When I told my father I was getting married, he looked at me with a sad smile.

'I'm very happy for you,' he said, 'but I will miss you a lot.'

I was swept up in the excitement of my engagement and gave no thought to my parents and how they would be feeling. I was looking forward to moving away from home, starting a new life and gaining some independence. We would be living only ten minutes away and I would still be a regular visitor.

But now I understand their loss, this shedding of children like layers of skin. My home is empty now. The house echoes because the rooms are bare, devoid of bodies and clutter. The silence is suffocating. I don't want to be alone with Steve, the four walls closing in around me. This should be our time for travel, for pursuing life's pleasures, for newfound freedom. Instead, we're both trapped by his illness.

Who am I now? I used to be the mother my children turned to for all their needs. I used to be the daughter of parents now long gone. I used to be the wife of a healthy, happy husband. I used to run a successful business. Now, I am a nurse whose days are punctuated by doses of medication and of mopping up bodily fluids. Now, I look after a patient who needs help showering, dressing, toileting, mobilising, and thinking. Now, I am an entertainment officer who directs each and every activity and who doubles as a chauffeur for multiple daily drives and doctors' appointments. Now, I am the chief cook, cleaner, gardener and home handy person. Now, I am someone's carer.

*

We are in the supermarket, shopping. Steve is hungry, so I give him five dollars and tell him to buy a sausage roll. I watch him walk out past the checkouts to the pie bar, just a few metres away. I get worried when he's out of my sight, so I hurry now, grabbing items quickly before heading to the checkout. I'm standing in the queue when I see him looking for me. I'm relieved to see him and wave, beckoning him. He joins me empty-handed.

'Where's your sausage roll?' I ask.

'They didn't have any,' he says. I'm taking items out of the trolley when a lady comes up to me and grabs my arm.

'I'm so glad he found you,' she says. 'I was standing with him at the pie bar but we couldn't work out what he wanted.' She is kind and compassionate, this stranger who has tried to help him.

I thank her and she hurries off to complete her shopping.

I buy him the sausage roll.

*

May 2012. We are sitting on a bench at Nobby's Beach. Steve is eating an ice cream – a Vanilla Heaven, his favourite. It's a beautiful May afternoon, unseasonably sunny and warm. The ocean is as blue as the sky and a young family is paddling in the shallows, the children shrieking with delight as each breaking wave dampens clothes. A grandmother with two little girls pad past on bare feet, an enthusiastic pair of young joggers pound the pavement, tanned and fit, and a group of young mothers push prams in the idyllic sunshine.

I see a couple approaching, a husband and wife. They are arm in arm but I notice that his gait does not match hers. I detect a slight shuffle and, as they come closer, I see a blank look on his face that is only too familiar. The woman is greying but is dressed youthfully in a skirt, top and sandals. Her husband has on long pants, shirt and jumper. He has a moustache, neatly trimmed, but he has a slightly shabby look. I wonder if she argued with him this morning about what he should wear or whether he feels the cold despite the warmth of the day.

They pause to have a drink from the bubbler, she first, then he following after. As they walk past our bench, she is smiling and chatting to him comfortably, keeping him stimulated and in touch with his environment. His face carries the expressionless countenance of a patient suffering brain failure. It is on the tip of my tongue to say something to her, because I see that she and I are travelling parallel paths. I want to tell her that I know. But I say nothing, because she is totally engrossed with her charge and her serene exterior suggests a peaceful acceptance that I do not yet possess. They walk on and she shepherds him across the road to the car park. She stops momentarily to read one of the plaques that provide historical information for the area, and, from a distance, it looks as though he, too, is engrossed. Then they disappear from sight.

I recognise us in that couple. I recognise the incapacitated husband with the vacant look, helpless, and dependent on his wife for both the simple and the complex activities of daily living. I recognise the devoted, loving wife who directs her husband through each day, prompting and encouraging his every move. Is this what we look like?

*

June 2012. The mouse scurries along the polished floorboards. It is running towards me as I sit reading. I see it out of the corner of my eye and raise my head, but it senses my sudden movement and stops, turns quickly and scuttles under the dining room table. I get up and circle the table in a wide arc. I'm nervous of this tiny furry creature, of its little pattering feet, of its speed as it criss-crosses my lounge room floor. I hurry into the kitchen and rummage in the back of a cupboard searching for a mousetrap. I find it – the old wooden type. It takes me a few minutes to work out how to set it. It snaps shut, narrowly missing my fingers as I try to prime it. Once, Steve would have set the trap but he is snoozing in the chair, unaware of the mouse and my fumbling attempts to get rid of it.

I can't sit in the lounge room now because I'm scared, so I wake Steve up, close the door, and go to bed safe in the knowledge that the mouse can't leave the room. I find the mouse in the trap the next morning. One glance tells me it's dead but I can't touch it and have to wait for a friend to dispose of it.

The next night, I hear the mouse before I see it. This one's more timid and it disappears quickly behind the curtain. This time, I'm prepared. I have set traps in every room just in case. I have also been hearing scratching noises in the ceiling and I'm worried there might be rats in the roof. When I go to bed, I hear scratching in my bedroom. I try sleeping in the spare room but the mice and the noises follow me from room to room. In desperation, I pull the blankets up over my head and finally fall asleep in the early hours of the morning. Steve sleeps soundly, undisturbed.

All the traps are empty but have been licked clean when I check them in the morning. I buy more traps, plastic ones this time, and as darkness falls, I smear peanut butter on them and set them ready in each room. I line them up meticulously a few centimetres away from each wall. Later, when I'm putting clothes away, I notice a small hole in the ceiling of the built-in wardrobe. Something has been chewing the gyprock. I find some steel wool and plug up the hole, but now I obsessively search every cupboard in every room. Any little cracks are blocked and towels are rolled up and put under doors. I feel as though I am being besieged by rodents. I am hyper-vigilant, unable to relax.

To allay my fears, Katie comes to stay overnight. It is past midnight when we go to bed. Katie, my protector, hops into the double bed with me. She falls asleep within minutes but I stay awake waiting for the noises to begin. Soon I hear the familiar scratching and then the rattle of the trap. I wait to hear it snap shut but all is quiet. I imagine the mouse scampering across the floor. I imagine it running up onto the bed and over me while I sleep. In the morning, we find a small grey mouse, its head clamped tightly in the trap. Why am I so terrorised by this tiny, defenceless animal? It's just a baby.

Three days pass and no more mice are caught. I begin to breathe more easily. A friend has helped me mouse-proof the house by making sure all possible entry points have been sealed. Ratsak has been put in the ceiling and I've heard no more scratching. It's a Saturday night and Steve has gone to bed when I feel a migraine threaten. I take my medication and fall into bed.

At six a.m., I'm woken by the rattle of the trap, then the squealing of the mouse. I put my fingers in my ears but still I hear the death throes as the mouse struggles in its final moments. Then silence as the darkness lifts and the soft light of a new winter's day starts filtering through the curtains. The house is quiet now – no mice scratching or traps rattling. Just the muted sound of Steve's gentle snoring permeating the early morning air.

*

August 2012. I cut the apple turnover in half. Apple and cream ooze out and my fingers are covered in icing sugar. I take it in on a plate for Steve and he enjoys this luscious sweet. He has lost weight recently so can afford a high-calorie treat. By the time he's finished, his mouth and fingers are covered in cream. I am relieved he's able to eat it because he often struggles with food these days. The food will sit in his mouth and he is unable to initiate chewing, making eating an arduous task. The pastry looks so delicious I eat the other half for afternoon tea.

Later that night, after dinner, Steve looks for something else to eat. I'm not sure what he's after so offer some suggestions. Would he like another sausage? A sandwich? Some ice cream? No. Then he mentions the word 'apple' and I offer to cut one up for him. But he doesn't want an apple. I finally understand that he wants the rest of the apple turnover and I confess, sheepishly, that I've eaten it. A crooked smile plays across his face and I giggle, too. Soon, we are both laughing uproariously over the incongruity of it all – this reversal of roles, where once he would have sneaked my treat and now I've eaten his. We stand together laughing over an apple turnover. And it feels so good.

*

September 2012. We are sitting in the car. It is raining, hardly the weather to be going out for a drive, but Steve is anxious to go somewhere, anywhere. He sits slumped, leaning over to one side, and I gently push him to straighten him up. A moment later, he is leaning again.

'Where do you want to go?' I ask.

His head is bowed and his voice muffled but I can just make out what he is saying. 'I want to see those people but I can't remember their names,' he says. 'I can't even remember your name.'

I am silent, shocked. 'You know who I am. I'm your wife, Linda.'

Relief crosses his face. He recognises the name and the familiarity is reassuring. He says nothing, but then I see tears roll down his cheek. They mingle with the saliva drooling from his mouth and his dripping nose.

I need to think of the right thing to say, something to ease his distress. Instead, I blurt out all the wrong things. I put him through a pointless test. 'Do you know who I am? Who are our daughters?'

He remembers one name, not the other.

I realise that in this instant he is aware: aware of his illness, aware of his loss, aware of what is happening to him. We sit together and weep.

'I'll be all right with you behind me,' he says, finally.

*

October 2012. For months, we have resisted. The occupational therapist has assessed and recommended, and we have finally agreed to try a hospital bed. Steve has been waking up with red areas on his hips, the result of recent weight loss, poor skin integrity and long periods at night spent lying in the one position. His reduced mobility makes him susceptible to pressure sores and I can no longer ignore the warning signs.

The OT is horrified when we show her how I help Steve in and out of bed. She worries I will injure myself. 'An electric bed will enable you to raise and lower the bed,' she tells me. 'We can put on a special mattress that will protect Steve from developing skin issues.'

We agree to a trial.

On the day of delivery, the OT waits with us for the bed to arrive. The van pulls into the drive and a young man in a neatly ironed green shirt and black pants alights with a concerned look on his face.

'I'm worried about the access,' he says.

We have steps and the bed we've been assigned does not pull apart. The man and the OT discuss options. The bed is heavy and hard to manoeuvre and they struggle getting through the front door and up the internal stairs. A friend has helped us dismantle our queen-size bed, I've vacuumed the dusty carpet and the room stands empty.

Finally, the bed is in position. With its levers, controls and cords, it looks like an alien spaceship landed in the middle of the room. The OT unwraps great sheaths of plastic from the blue vinyl mattress and places it on the metal frame.

Steve stands behind me and whispers that he doesn't want the bed.

'Let's try it,' I say. 'We don't have to keep it if you don't like it.'

This mechanical device, so impersonal and practical, symbolises the progression of his disease. I don't want the bed either.

The first night, I raise the head of the bed and Steve lies on his back all night. The mattress feels hard and unyielding but he doesn't complain. In the morning, he groans when I help him out of bed; he hasn't slept well. The second night, he lies on his side. When he wakes in the morning, he has a large angry-looking red area on his hip.

I ring the OT. 'The mattress isn't any good,' I wail. I describe the red patch and Steve's discomfort.

The OT tells me we can try another mattress but I am despondent.

'I don't want the bed,' I blubber. 'I was trying to help him and now I've just made things worse.'

The OT listens to my outburst and tries to soothe me. 'We'll try something else,' she says. 'I'll have the bed collected. The red patch will go away.'

We talk until I calm down but we both know my real distress is about Steve becoming sicker.

A few days later, the bed is collected. The removal is even more problematic than the delivery, and it takes several attempts to manhandle the bed down the stairs and out to the truck. I stand at the front door and watch as the bed disappears from sight. Back inside, I examine the chipped banister rail, a casualty of the whole process and a reminder of what the future holds.

*

December 2012. I am lying in bed, reading, when my right forefinger starts twitching. I watch it move from side to side. Its movement is completely involuntary and I have no control over its action. I sit up in bed, frantic. I think of Michael J. Fox. He woke up one morning with a twitching finger and the diagnosis was Parkinson's disease.

I lie back on the pillows and try to steady my breathing. Since Steve's condition has progressed, I've become hyper-alert to medical symptoms. Aches and pains invariably have a sinister cause; tingling or muscle twitching always stem from a neurological basis. I've noticed some weakness in my hand and I worry that I have MS or motor neurone disease. I stay awake long into the night, imagining the worst.

The doctor looks me straight in the eye and says, 'It's not Parkinson's.' She is used to my fears and paranoia. She checks the function of my hand and arm and asks if I have experienced any numbness. She thinks I may have some nerve impingement in my wrist and orders a carpel tunnel test. 'Don't lose any sleep over it,' she says, but I still worry obsessively about a possible dire diagnosis.

The carpel tunnel test is conducted a month later at a neurologist's rooms.

The technician performs the test. 'The nerves in your hand and wrist are healthy,' he tells me. 'I can't find any problem.' He tells me to wait, that the neurologist will come in to discuss the results with me.

The neurologist enters the room ten minutes later. He is a warm, friendly man about my age. He holds my hand and checks its range of movement. We discuss my painful thumbs (probably arthritis) and the fact that the test hasn't shown up any nerve problem.

'What caused the twitching?' I ask, and he shrugs. 'Stuff happens!' he says.

The twitching, tingling and soreness disappear overnight.

*

January 2013. We top the crest of the hill and the magnificent view across Port Stephens stretches out before us. Every January, for thirty years, we have camped at Jimmy's Beach Caravan Park, Hawks Nest. Steve loves camping and has been coming here since he was a child when the punt was the only way to cross the river from Tea Gardens to Hawks Nest. Now, a concrete bridge spans the water, affording views of the oyster farms when the tide is low. Occasionally, dolphins frolic here. The small riverside township of Tea Gardens with its mix of trendy eateries and family-friendly ice cream parlours and fish and chip shops is a hive of activity in the holiday season. Hawks Nest is more laid-back; a bakery, newsagent and takeaway shop dominate the main street. After thirty years, nothing much has changed.

Yacaaba on the Hawks Nest side and Tomaree on the Nelson Bay side are imposing headlands that frame the opening to the bay. On a clear day, with blue skies reflected in the pristine waters of the ocean and bay, it is hard to imagine a more beautiful area of coastline anywhere in the world. We have always preferred the quieter, less commercial area of Hawks Nest. With access to both the bay and the ocean, it has provided an idyllic holiday destination for family and friends over the years.

The caravan park has been recently renovated. For years, the park consisted of old vans and humpies alongside crowded rows of holidaymakers in tents and caravans. There was no boom gate, tennis court or swimming pool. The main amenities block was near the entrance and the 'bush toilets' were situated at the other end of the park. It was a no-frills experience.

Eventually, the Great Lakes Shire Council decided that the electrical wiring needed replacing and that the park was a fire hazard and occupational health and safety risk. Although the residents and regular customers resisted, the park was closed for twelve months while repairs and improvements were implemented. For years, we had joked and complained about the dated amenities block with its 1970s brown-patterned tiles and broken showerheads. We would sit on the long bench waiting for a free shower cubicle and count the cobwebs on the ceiling.

Now, the amenities block has been modernised with white tiles and keypad entry. But some things never change. When I have my shower, I see a dark brown cockroach halfway up the wall. I wonder if it is semi-comatose from the heat and steam. It's there, in the same spot, every night.

Most of the permanent van sites have been removed and the camping ground has a quieter atmosphere now. There are no late-night revelries any more. Although many of the residents were elderly and kept to themselves, the alcohol used to flow freely in some quarters. Groups of four-wheel drive enthusiasts and fishermen would celebrate the end of long, hot summer days. These devotees of beer-drinking and card-playing would party on well into the warm, balmy nights.

The caravan park has a new manager and a new image. The emphasis is on families now and a new camp kitchen and open grassed area stand in the centre of the park. On the lower level, a movie screen is erected on Sunday nights and a crowd gathers on the lawn to watch. One night, a singer, a male in his fifties, provides the entertainment. He's a one-man show with an impressive repertoire of popular and country songs. A group of ladies, champagne glasses in hand, are up dancing. Children are laughing and running around. I sit on my camp chair in an open theatre, under a starry night, and drink in the music.

Our tent is almost thirty years old. We bought it when I was pregnant with Sally. We stood in the camping shop and imagined our young family in that tent. It would be big enough for four. A zipped-up area at one end would be the bedroom, and the other room would provide storage. It is the old canvas type, strong and sturdy. There are a couple of small holes here and there and the roof is stained with sap from the trees, but it is still waterproof, providing protection from the rain and wind.

We camp with our friends the Martyns. I have known Jill since she was eight years old and a student in my ballet school. We've been friends with Phil, an industrial arts teacher like Steve, since he married Jill more than twenty years ago. The Martyns live inland and look forward to their coastal holiday every summer. Years ago, Phil constructed the 'Taj Mahal,' a framework of poles with a tarpaulin roof. It provides a shaded area between the two tents where we can sit and relax, prepare meals and shelter from the weather.

This will be our last year at Jimmy's Beach. Camping with Steve is too hard now. We sleep on foam mattresses on the floor and it's almost impossible to get him up off the ground. The toilets are the other problem.

When we check in, I ask the manager for a key to the disabled bathroom. The office is busy and he appears flustered.

He looks us up and down and asks, 'Who is the disabled person here?'

I look at him in disbelief and point to Steve.

The manager's voice is loud and aggressive when he asks, 'What's wrong with him?'

I'm angry now; surely Steve's condition is obvious. 'He has Parkinson's disease,' I answer, my voice clipped.

The manager appears taken aback and he presents us with the key but I'm ready to get in the car and drive home. It's the first time I've encountered rudeness of this kind – most people are sympathetic.

Unlike the old 'bush toilets' which were directly opposite our campsite, the new toilets are too far away from our tent and I need to put Steve in the car and drive him to the disabled toilet in the main amenities block. He can't find his way back to the tent site if I let him go on his own and it is too far to walk. His eyes struggle to stay open against the glare of bright sunny weather. The days are long and hot and he is unable to nap or rest adequately.

For the first time, Steve is ambivalent about the camping experience and is happy to go home for rest days. I have never wholeheartedly embraced our camping holidays, tolerating this yearly event only because Steve and the family enjoyed it. The sand, mosquitoes, sandflies, sunburn, rain, noisy neighbours and public amenities have, at times, been hard to endure. Yet camping is part of our history together, of family traditions, of the sharing of laughter and, sometimes, sadness with our friends, and of watching our children grow.

As we fold up the tent for the last time, I am overcome with nostalgia. Images of three-year-old Katie on her little blue trike rattling along the gravel road flash through my mind. Later, when our girls were teenagers, they would bring friends along. One year, we had eight girls to look after. We cooked and ate in two shifts and everyone piled into the four-wheel drives for days on the beach. I also remember the smelly wet towels hung under the Taj Mahal on rainy days, the wet, black sand walked through tents and into beds, the packing and unpacking, the interminable loads of washing.

One night, towards the end of our holiday, we head to the bay to watch the sunset. We buy takeaway fish and chips for dinner and sit on our camping chairs looking out over the water. Families are still in swimming or paddling. A few fishermen are trying their luck. The sun is still high in the sky when Steve starts getting restless. He has eaten his meal and is ready to move. His concentration span is so short now that nothing occupies him for long. We distract him by taking a little walk along the shoreline, letting the water wash over our feet, feeling the sand between our toes.

We see a group of boys and girls, in their late teens, laughing and talking. They are celebrating the end of their school years and I envy their youth and their dreams. I remember being their age and having a future to look forward to. Our future looms uncertainly now, unchartered territory that frightens me. I feel the familiar rising panic that washes over me from time to time. I breathe deeply, trying to focus on the moment, here on the beach, with our friends, on this beautiful evening.

The sky is changing now. The sun is setting amid a riot of orange and pink. It is a glowing ball dropping quickly and I stand spellbound. Then, all too soon, it dips below the horizon and the sky fades. Steve is impatient, so we pack up. The others walk on ahead but I trail behind, reluctant to leave the beach, the sunset, and this chapter in our lives.

*

February 2013. I am worn out by my carer duties but the prospect of future residential care is unthinkable. I don't discuss this topic with Steve. The doctors and Parkinson's nurse broach the subject with us both. I see the fear in Steve's eyes.

*

I take Steve to a younger-onset group for people with cognitive problems. It is a mixed group, male and female, and all participants are under the age of sixty-five. I see that the other members of the group are in better health than Steve. Most can still carry out good conversations, play cards or dominoes, and interact easily with each other. On first glance, and if I didn't know better, I wouldn't guess that some of them have memory problems. But as I become more acquainted with this eclectic group, the cracks and fissures soon appear. A blank look here, an inability to find the correct word there, and I recognise the familiar signs.

The group is run by an enthusiastic young man, whose calm demeanour and affable personality make him instantly likeable. He welcomes Steve each week with genuine warmth, as though he could think of nothing nicer than to enjoy my husband's company. I'm also made to feel welcome, even though there are no other carers present. Steve is an unwilling participant; he never asks to go but I drive him there each week anyway. Then I hover like an overprotective mother, reluctant to leave. I wonder whether the staff are silently cursing my presence.

One week, everyone is asked to bring in a brief autobiography. As we sit around the table, the bios are read out. One man worked as a distinguished pathologist in a large hospital, another worked as a cleaner. Yet another is a keen fisherman and has an avid interest in birds. All led productive lives, had spouses and children, and futures to look forward to. There is shared respect around the table for each life history and for the joys and sorrows, losses and achievements. The onset of illness in their forties and fifties has disrupted lives and plans, but not crushed spirits. There is laughter too.

If the weather is fine, a game of bocce is organised in the back garden. The garden is shaded by leafy trees. Paths meander through the lush green lawn and garden beds add vibrant colour. There is an outdoor eating area with a barbecue and wooden furniture. A small gazebo graces one corner of the yard. A gravel path becomes the bowling alley and the small red ball is placed down one end ready for play.

The participants line up. Each player is given a silver ball with a number so that play can progress in an orderly fashion. If the group is big, two teams are formed so that everyone can have a turn. Steve is encouraged to go outside and play. Last week, he refused to take part, but today he goes happily. I stay inside and watch through the window.

Three women and three men are playing today. There is camaraderie amongst the players with much laughing and cheering when someone manages a good throw. One of the women is in her early sixties. She is a tall woman with grey hair and a ruddy complexion. I notice that she is helping Steve, telling him when it's his turn to play and taking him by the hand and positioning him at the end of the path. Then she guides him back to his seat when he's had his turn. It's a warm day and she has a red face when she comes inside. Then I notice that she's crying. 'It's not fair,' I hear her say. 'He's a nice man. This shouldn't be happening to him.'

It takes me a few moments to realise she's talking about Steve. One of the carers consoles her and I tell her not to worry about Steve, that he has lots of people who love him and look after him. It takes some minutes before she is composed again. I met her husband at the group one day. He told me how she becomes very frustrated at home when she is unable to remember how to perform household duties. The reversal of roles when he takes over the housework makes her angry. Her husband is still working. 'I couldn't stay at home and look after her full-time,' he told me. 'I'd go crazy.'

There is no sign of her anger now. Her red eyes and tear-stained face reflect her empathy and grief for another's suffering. Her emotional outburst on behalf of my husband is touching.

*

I press the buzzer. Through the screen door, I see a long hallway with floorboards polished to a high sheen. The hall opens out onto a dining room and I can see people seated at a long table. It is twelve thirty – lunchtime – and I wonder if I have arrived at an inconvenient time.

Then I hear a female voice saying, 'I'll get the door,' and a tiny bird-like woman bustles down the hall towards me. She unlocks the screen door and holds it open for me.

'I'm looking for some respite care for my husband,' I hear myself say. 'Is it okay if I have a look around?'

She ushers me in, explaining that it's party day today for all the February birthdays. I can smell sausage rolls and tomato sauce. But there is no laughter or chatter at this birthday party, just silence as the elderly patients sit quietly eating. Some gaze vacantly into space, others look up from their food as I arrive. I avoid their blank faces and wish I could turn around and run back out through that front door.

But I don't run. Instead, I allow the manager to show me through the cottage. She explains that these are day patients but she can also offer overnight respite care. The house consists of three bedrooms with en suites, a separate larger bathroom, an open plan kitchen, dining and lounge room area and two offices.

The bedrooms are sparsely furnished with timber floors. I try to picture Steve in one of the narrow single beds and voice my concern about his difficulties getting into and out of bed. At home, we have a routine. He is able to climb into the queen bed but I need to raise the pillows and position them under his neck. I pull his arm to release his shoulder from an uncomfortable position. Then I have to arrange his legs so they don't rub together. Finally, I pull the sheets and blankets up. When I know that he is resting comfortably, I kiss him goodnight. How can I leave him to total strangers to complete these rituals?

Sometimes, he needs to get up during the night. At home, I hear him and can help him out of bed. I am told there is only one carer on duty at night but am assured that regular checks are done throughout the night. I hate the thought of him lying in a strange bed in a strange room waiting for someone to help him up. Or worse, what if he tries to get out by himself and, disorientated, falls to the floor? The manager tells me they can give him a buzzer to press but we both know he won't remember to use it.

The bathrooms have toilet images on the doors but I suspect Steve will have trouble finding the toilet in these unfamiliar surroundings. I'm told the patients are toileted on a regular basis, but sometimes Steve has trouble getting to the bathroom on time even when he's at home.

We walk back out into the living area. All the meals are cooked here in the kitchen. There is a young woman standing at the sink. She is a dark-haired girl, perhaps in her twenties, tall and slim. At first, I think she is one of the helpers. Then I realise she is one of the patients. She comes to the centre three days a week to give her parents a break. I can't determine from this brief encounter what her problem is or why she has to spend her days in the company of the elderly. She smiles at me, unperturbed.

The living room opens onto an outdoor area and we go outside. The manager talks to me about everything the centre has on offer, the way they try to accommodate the patient's needs and why the patient comes first. Her words wash over me, but I am no longer listening. It's a very warm, humid day and after a few minutes I start to feel faint in the oppressive heat. There's no doubt that I desperately need a break from the demands of looking after Steve but I cannot leave him in the care of strangers. He would hate it and I would be racked with guilt.

I am led back through the house to the front door. We walk through the cool air-conditioned rooms but I feel the perspiration trickling down between my breasts and shoulder blades. Little beads of sweat coat my upper lip.

We stand at the front door and I am told I must look after myself, that if I don't take care of myself there will be no one to take care of Steve. I have heard this advice before – many times – and I nod. But I know that I won't be bringing Steve here. And the manager knows it too.

*

We are walking on the boardwalk at Redhead Beach. It is a warm afternoon but the sea breeze cools us. It will be a short walk today because Steve is slow and confused. He has slept in and I have finally woken him at midday. It takes him another hour and a half to have his breakfast and shower and he's still sluggish when I put him in the car and drive to the beach.

We visit Redhead Beach regularly. The beach was always a favourite haunt. Steve was a strong swimmer and enjoyed the surf. I can still see him catching a wave on his boogie board and surf ski. He even spent some time as a volunteer surf lifesaver. Now, I'm afraid to let him go in the water because his balance is impaired and his eyes close when they get water in them. The surf is too dangerous for him and his body too vulnerable, but we're still able to enjoy the beach atmosphere and go for regular walks on the sand or along the boardwalk.

As we finish our walk and trudge back up the hill to the car park, I see a man and dog approaching. I usher Steve in front of me so the man can get past us on the narrow path. I lower my eyes as the man passes. I am always self-conscious when walking with Steve, worried that he is drooling, that his mouth is open, or that he has food stains on the front of his T-shirt. The man stops to talk. He is young, of indistinguishable age, his skin smooth and tanned. Despite his youthful appearance, his hair is greying.

He looks at Steve as though he knows him well and asks, 'How are you going? Are you keeping okay?' He holds his hand out and shakes Steve's hand.

'Are you an ex-student?' I ask. We are often accosted by past students who have remembered Steve from their schooldays.

The man shakes his head and I realise he is a total stranger who has stopped to talk. 'How are you doing?' he asks again.

Steve gives his usual response, 'I'm a bit slow,' but he's smiling now.

I nod. 'Steve has some problems, but at least we're able to get out for a walk.'

The man smiles at us both and then we talk about his dog – small talk. Buddy is as gentle as his owner and stands obediently as we chat. Then the moment is over and we move apart.

'Well, have a good day,' he says.

I watch as he and Buddy head off down the path. I am smiling as I walk back to the car.

*

March 2013. Steve is eating his dinner. He is sitting in his chair, a serviette tucked into his shirt. The plate is placed on a stable table on his lap. Eating at the dining room table is difficult because he can't manoeuvre the chair in close enough. When we eat out, we often have to move the table over for him so that he can eat in a more comfortable position.

Tonight, I have cooked pasta. I stir the mince sauce through the small pasta shells. Then I grate cheese over the meal. Steve has been having trouble chewing his food, so I've been cooking soft foods with lots of gravies and sauces. His inability to chew means that sometimes he has to spit food out. He has lost weight.

I watch him move the spoon slowly to his mouth. I encourage him to eat small mouthfuls but he has piled the food onto the spoon. He opens his mouth and puts a spoonful in. Sometimes, he is able to get his mouth moving and he chews and swallows with ease. At other times, the food just sits in his mouth. I remind him to chew and sometimes that triggers a response. Another spoonful will also sometimes generate the chewing response. I urge him to have a sip of water to help the process.

If nothing else works, I plead with him to start chewing and he hears the exasperation in my voice. He stares at me with accusing eyes but I become desperate. There is a risk of choking or of aspirating the food if he can't chew and swallow. But an even greater fear is that his inability to eat will lead to more drastic measures. If he can't eat, he will eventually need a feeding peg inserted into his stomach so that nutrients may be administered. I don't want him to go through this invasive procedure with its limitations and risk of infection. Steve was always a hearty eater who enjoyed his food. Now every meal generates anxiety.

I take the spoon from his hands and start feeding him small mouthfuls. He manages a little better but soon wants to take the spoon back into his own hands. I can't blame him. I seem to have taken control of every aspect of his life. The last vestiges of independence are slowly disappearing and he tries valiantly to feed himself. I see the food sit in his mouth and the saliva spilling out and dribbling onto the plate. He is slouched over now and refuses any more food. I take the plate away and wipe his mouth clean with a paper towel. Another towel wipes the red pasta sauce from his T-shirt.

Then I spit out the unforgiveable, 'You need a nurse, not a wife!'

He gazes at me in silent reproach, his eyes unwavering, and I slink off to the kitchen to drown my frustration and sorrow in a sink full of dirty dishes.

*

Snip, snip, snip. The point of the scissors edges around the curves of the pattern and through two layers of satin. I peel the paper off and feel the silky smoothness of the material. It slips between my fingers as I weave the pins in and out. Now I cut strips of tulle. The netting is delicate and crushes softly as I gather it in my hands.

I work methodically, cutting, pinning, tacking, sewing. The bodice goes together easily. I press the darts and seams, carefully guiding the iron over its shiny surface. The tulle is more difficult. It is voluminous and delicate. I use long stitches to gather the netting. Sometimes the stitches snap as I pull on the gathering threads. It is fiddly, time-consuming work making sure the gathering is even. I guide the material into soft folds and fit the skirt to the bodice. The garment goes together perfectly – it is soft, dainty, ethereal.

We are preparing for Sally's wedding and I am sewing the flower girl dresses. I concentrate on the beauty of my creation and the texture of the fabric beneath my hands.

Earlier my hands had showered the excrement from Steve's body and legs. I'd left him with his father for an hour and when I returned found him outside standing on the driveway, his pants dirtied, his fingers caked in faeces. Inside, his elderly father was cleaning up the trail of waste propelled from his son's body.

I put towels on the car seat and we drive home, the windows open. We are both silent. His shoes are soiled and I make him take them off at the front door. I guide him to the bathroom and help him undress. He stands in the shower, the hot water rinsing him clean. He allows me access to the private parts of his body as I lather up the soap and wash him. I wonder what he is thinking.

I wrap his dirty underwear in a plastic bag and throw it in the bin. I bundle up the clothes and towels and put them in the washing machine. I put the shoes out on the lawn and turn the hose on. I wipe the car door handles with disinfectant. I scrub the shower recess and mop the bathroom floor. I spray air freshener throughout the house.

I pick up the dress and hold it out in front of me. I imagine two little flower girls in ivory. I see them twirling around, the frothy cream tulle floating out as they spin. I see the flowers in their hair and baskets of rose petals in their hands as they walk down the aisle. I see the sun shining.

I put the dress back on its hanger, carefully arranging the tulle so it drapes softly. Then I close the door and walk back down the hall to Steve.

*

The ice cream dribbles down Steve's chin and onto his T-shirt. He is eating a soft-serve cone and it's melting rapidly. I tell him to eat quickly, to lick around the edges as the white creamy substance threatens to spill.

We are sitting in the car park at McDonald's. This is a regular haunt and a regular treat. When my mother was in a nursing home, the elderly residents would sometimes be taken out in the bus and stop for a Macca's ice cream. She loved going out on the bus – at least, I think she did. She lost the ability to express herself in those last three years. She went off on the bus and I went home to my own little family, relieved that someone else was responsible for her care. My mother was elderly and frail and I worried about her constantly. I visited her every day, fed her lunch, made sure she had everything she needed. I surrounded her with love.

That was almost twenty years ago. Now, I am taking Steve for drives and buying him ice creams. The melting ice cream leaves sticky patches on his shorts and on the seat belt. It runs down his arm. I wipe his hands and chin. I don't have enough tissues or serviettes and my hands are sticky too. I become annoyed. It's like looking after a three-year-old.

One day, he whispers to me, 'I'm just like a little kid.' He needs help with most things now. The disease is robbing him of all his skills, big and small – even of eating an ice cream.

*

April 2013. 'Lost'. He has written the word twice, under the juice, bread, bicarb soda, peppercorns and rubber gloves on my shopping list. I recognise Steve's spidery handwriting with its long loops. The top word is well-formed, the second frail and wavery. I'm surprised he can still write and even more surprised he can still spell.

I have been out and have been away much longer than planned. When I return, I find him wandering the house half undressed. He has taken his socks, shoes and shorts off and I see he has taken a clean T-shirt out of the drawer and has laid it out on the bed. He can't tell me why, or why the washing-up detergent and scourer are in the fridge.

After I help him dress, we stand in the kitchen and look at the shopping list. 'Why did you write "lost"?' I ask.

'I thought you were lost,' he says.

I see the bemused look on his face and realise we are both lost. He flounders in a sea of confusion and delusions. I am drowning in an ocean of fear and uncertainty, in turn engulfed by waves and resurfacing to catch my breath.

*

A new worrying spot appears on Steve's head and I am distraught. He is put on precautionary antibiotics to protect him from infection. The antibiotics are large capsules in two shades of green and Steve has trouble swallowing them. I cajole, threaten and demand they be swallowed, all to no avail. He spits the capsule and its half-dissolved contents out into the bathroom sink and I see that the plastic coating has left him with a green tongue. I can't be sure how much of the medication has been absorbed, so we try again with another capsule, again without success. I am angry now and break open a third capsule and mix the contents with some apricot yoghurt. He finally swallows it but we are both upset as I help him get ready for bed. I turn off the light in silence without the customary goodnight kiss.

I am sitting quietly reading when I hear him. He has turned on the bedroom light and is waiting for me. When I ask him what's wrong, he wraps his arms around me in a tight hug, our heads close.

'I just wanted to say goodnight,' he mumbles into my shoulder. His hold is forgiving.

*

I step into the elevator. It is six thirty p.m. Earlier today, Steve had an appointment with the neurosurgeon, who diagnosed the spot as a possible infection of the wires. Steve sat in the car and cried after the appointment, overwhelmed at the thought of another operation. Now he has been admitted into North Shore Private Hospital and is awaiting surgery on the affected area in two days' time. He will then need to be on lifelong antibiotics. I have come to Sydney prepared for a possible hospitalisation and have brought his clothes and medications. It has been a long, stressful day and I am worried that the planned treatment won't cure the infection. I am on my way home to Newcastle and will return tomorrow.

The neurosurgeon is in the elevator. He has just completed his rounds of the ward. He rides with me down to the ground floor. 'How old is Steve?' he asks.

'Fifty-eight,' I answer, and I see the sympathy in his eyes. 'The infection will keep recurring, won't it?' I worry, and the doctor shakes his head.

'Not if we keep him on antibiotics,' he tells me.

But I am unconvinced, remembering the last infection, the failed antibiotics and the removal of the wires.

Perhaps he reads my mind, because now the doctor says, 'I think Steve would soon pass away if the wires had to be removed.'

I can't speak. The lift door opens and I step out onto the polished marble floor. The doctor tells me he will see me after the operation and I walk out into the cool of the evening. It is still light as I make my way to the car park. I put the key in the ignition and point the car in the direction of home. I weave in and out of the Sydney traffic and the rush of cars on the freeway. The conversation with the doctor stays with me all the way home.

*

An unexpected gift: the night before surgery Steve grabs my arm and says, 'Thanks for being here. Take care of yourself.'

*

Good news! The surgeon tells us there is no sign of an infection. He has removed the spot and cleansed the area. Steve will be on intravenous antibiotics for a few days and then allowed home. We are all overjoyed. Now we can look forward to Sally's wedding, just a few weeks away.

*

May 2013.

>Dear Sally,
>
>Today is your wedding day. I didn't sleep a wink last night – excitement, anticipation, and nervous energy kept me awake. I turned the light on and did some reading, ate an apple (my mother's remedy for insomnia), tried counting backwards from five hundred in threes, but nothing worked. During the night, the wind blew, the branches on the shrub outside the bedroom window scratching the roof tiles. Then I thought I heard rain and started

worrying that your beautiful gown would get wet and that the outdoor wedding ceremony would have to be conducted indoors. I uttered a silent prayer – please let it be sunny tomorrow.

Finally, just after five thirty a.m, I get out of bed and walk through the silent house. The first signs of a grey dawn are emerging but I switch on lights and turn the heater on. I hear you stir at six a.m. and you come out of the bedroom in your warm dressing gown, your hair tousled from a restless night. You give me a hug and I hold you close. You have that familiar 'just woken up' smell I remember from your childhood.

'Today is your wedding day,' I whisper into your ear, as if to remind myself that it's really happening, that my baby girl is all grown up. You smile a radiant smile. It's over four years since you've slept in your childhood bed but you came home yesterday to spend the night with us. Your bridesmaids came for dinner and we all stayed up late talking and laughing. We painted toenails, shared memories and revelled in the excitement of preparing for your wedding. We've followed all the traditional rituals – the kitchen tea, the hen's party, the garter, the something old, something new, something borrowed, something blue, the bridal gown, the train, the veil.

Last night, your father sat in his chair silent, dozing on and off. I'm not sure how aware he is of this momentous occasion. Does he understand that it's your wedding, one of the most important days in your life? I've talked to him about it often, offering constant reminders, but he rarely responds. Perhaps he does realise. If he'd been well, he would have been excited too. I don't let your father's unresponsiveness upset me. I want to enjoy every moment of your wedding. I need to be happy too.

At six thirty a.m., the hairdresser arrives. The family room becomes a makeshift hair salon as we sit on stools looking out the window at the lightening sky. The room is filled with chatter and laughter. The hairdresser works quickly, straightening, curling, blow drying, and teasing every strand of hair. After my hair is styled, I make ham and cheese croissants and coffee and you all eat hungrily. I keep checking on your dad, who is still asleep. When he wakes, we go through our usual morning routine – pills, breakfast, shower, getting dressed. What is normally a tedious regime flies by this morning. 'Today is Sally's wedding,' I tell him and I think he understands.

Soon it is time to leave for the beautician. Yesterday, my fingernails were filed, buffed, painted and polished. Today, I sit on a stool as my make-up is applied. The beautician blends colours and hues until the canvas of my face is transformed. I gaze into the mirror and see a stranger. Her skin is flawless, her cheeks highlighted, her lips full, her eyes luminous. I can barely recognise myself and worry that the make-up is too heavy and too dramatic. But I love the glamour. It is all part of the magic of the day and I allow myself to be primped and preened and to enjoy the luxury of feeling beautiful.

Your father's transformation is also about to begin. The personal care assistant shaves your dad and dresses him in his dark suit. He has on a pale blue shirt and navy tie to match my dress and he looks so handsome. Gone are the T-shirt, windcheater, tracksuit pants and joggers that have been his uniform for years now. He can no longer do up buttons or zippers, but we can deal with that. He will have to wear incontinence pants but no one will know. He will dribble and spill his food but it doesn't matter. Today, he will fulfil his role as father of the bride and we will treasure every moment.

The bridal gown, bridesmaids, flower girl and mother of the bride dresses are all hanging in the spare bedroom. Every item for your wedding has been lovingly chosen and placed here – your dress, veil, shoes and jewellery. All the accessories for my outfit are here too – the navy satin shoes that so perfectly match my dress, the borrowed clutch bag, the beaded wrap, the earrings and bracelet. Sometimes, I stand in this room and savour the beauty of these exquisite items.

It is time to help you dress. Your wedding gown is a vision in ivory satin and tulle, the bodice embroidered with sparkling crystals. We carefully lift the delicate garment over your head and then lace up the corset, pulling the ribbon tight. The voluminous skirt of satin and tulle sweeps from your waist into a short train. You call it a 'princess dress' and you look like a princess. Your hair is swept up into soft curls that sit above the nape of your neck and the beaded hairpiece and creamy veil frame your face.

Your wedding ceremony is being held on the deck of a seaside resort and when we arrive, fashionably late, the guests are waiting. My wish has come true – the sun is shining and, in the background, the ocean is a brilliant blue. Your father holds your hand and, together, you walk down the aisle. I hold my breath, worried he will stumble or trip over your dress. But this short walk, that holds so much meaning for our family, is without incident. When your dad was first diagnosed, you were only seventeen and I worried then that he might be too ill to ever walk you down the aisle. Now, he delivers you safely to your groom and we give our blessing on your marriage.

As the celebrant begins the ceremony, a cold wind springs up. It starts gently at first then becomes stronger, the gusts catching beneath your veil and flattening the front of your dress. White caps dot the ocean as the clouds roll in. Your vows are completed and you are man and wife. Nothing can dampen your joy or disturb your composure. While I shiver in my summer dress, silently cursing the arctic wind, you brim with happiness. The wedding guests gather round to congratulate you but soon the wind drives them indoors and you leave to have your photos taken.

The reception is held in a function room in the resort. It is a large room with high ceilings and modern decor but the atmosphere is warm and welcoming. The tables are covered with white tablecloths, the chairs adorned with ivory sashes. At the centre of each table is a tall champagne glass with crystals cascading from the rim. After the guests are seated, the bridal party makes its entrance. You are beaming as you take your place at the head table. A nurse has come to help me look after your dad and she cuts his food and encourages him to eat. Her presence is reassuring and I'm able to relax and enjoy the meal and the night. You cut the cake and then it's time for the speeches. I make my way to the microphone and deliver the parent of the bride speech. I talk about our love for you, how proud we are of you, and our hopes for you as you enter your marriage. My voice catches and I see the tears roll down your cheeks. But tonight all the tears are happy tears.

Then we are on the dance floor. You dance with your father and I think how quickly the years have passed since our own wedding. I remember dancing the bridal waltz with your dad. We look so young in the photos – just twenty-five and our whole lives ahead of us. We were both leaving our childhood homes, starting out on a big adventure together. We left the wedding reception in our old Corolla with 'Just Married' in shaving cream plastered across the rear window and cans and streamers tied to the bumper bar. Our honeymoon was a road trip to Brisbane. We'd just bought our first home. I remember the excitement of buying that house. It was brand-new, a spec home. We started with Mum and Dad's old lounge, a mattress on the floor and a card table for the dining room. We saved hard and soon bought a wall unit, a dining table and an ensemble for the bedroom. I made curtains for every room. I was proud of that little house and cried five years later when we moved.

The nurse takes your father home when the official part of the reception is over, but I stay on. All too soon, the night comes to an end. The wedding day we have planned for, looked forward to, and dreamed about, is over. You are now a married woman and life with your new husband has just begun. For us as your parents, a part of our life is over.

I walk out into a moonless night, the icy wind chilling me as I pull my wrap closer around me. My teeth are chattering as I slip my high heels off and run to the car. I hear the roar of the ocean and the waves breaking on the shore. Then I look up at the stars sparkling brightly in the inky sky and I pray that all your hopes and dreams come true.

Love,
Mum xx

*

Two weeks after the wedding, Steve develops an infection on his scalp that is related to, and potentially hazardous to, his deep brain stimulators. Within days, he has surgical debridement of the infected area. He stays in Sydney for the surgery and then the follow-up intravenous antibiotic treatment. I commute to Sydney daily, dreading the two-hour drive. I arrive at midday and leave in the evening for the long trip home, arriving to a cold, empty house.

After a week, Steve is transferred back to a local hospital. He arrives by patient transport and is exhausted from the journey. The look of relief on his face when he sees me breaks my heart. The surgery, anaesthetic and subsequent treatment have been a major setback and his condition is poor. The wound on his head is healing but no one knows if the treatment will hold the infection at bay.

Steve needs an intravenous drip to administer his antibiotics. The technician arrives to insert a PICC line deep into his chest. The line is inserted through his arm and Steve lies on his back, his arm outstretched as the technician searches for a vein. She is using an ultrasound to locate the best vein for insertion of the line. Then all the instruments are carefully laid out ready for the procedure. The technician and her assistant are well-practised and I am impressed with their professionalism and reassuring manner.

Steve lies quietly with his eyes closed as they prepare him. He is praised for his good behaviour and the calm way in which he accepts this latest invasion into his body. Then he opens his eyes and the technician gives him a warm smile. Steve smiles back and I am suddenly sad. I see the old Steve, the friendly, outgoing man he used to be.

I leave the ward in tears. I need a moment but there is no private space for weeping, nowhere to get away from nurses, patients, visitors. I stand in a corner, my back to the general public but I feel a hand on my back.

'Are you okay?' a stranger asks. I wipe my eyes and the woman says sympathetically, 'It sucks, doesn't it?'

Two days later, Steve forgets that the line in his chest is attached to an antibiotic drip and gets up out of his chair. The PICC line is yanked from his chest and leaves a trail of blood behind him as he walks around the ward.

*

June 2013. While Steve is in hospital, the house feels empty. I move aimlessly through the vacant rooms unable to focus on the simplest of tasks. I worry about him alone in the hospital, unable to communicate his needs. I worry about the level of care and the timing and dosage of his tablets. I visit him daily spending long hours in the neurology ward.

I need to keep the hospitalisation as stress-free as possible for him but I also need to reassure myself.

One evening, Katie convinces me to go out for dinner. I leave the hospital early, before Steve goes to sleep, and we drive to a local restaurant. The dark, intimate interior of the eatery contrasts with the bright white hospital ward and I sit on the edge of my chair, awkward and unpractised in this environment. The restaurant is busy and noisy and we are wedged into a small space near other diners. The confinement is close and claustrophobic. Later, when I arrive home, I see the red light flashing on my answering machine. There is a message from a nurse at the hospital telling me Steve has refused his bedtime tablets. The nurse asks for my help. It is now nine-thirty, long past medication time, but I ring the ward and speak to the nurse, who tells me that Steve eventually swallowed his tablets.

Steve is in a four-bed ward with curtains dividing the room. There is little privacy. One night, a patient is admitted who clearly suffers from a mental health problem. He is confined to the bed and assigned a nurse to keep watch. The side rails on the bed are up and the man tries constantly to escape his prison.

'Stay in bed,' the nurse warns him as he struggles to climb out.

The man keeps asking the time, and then in his frustration starts swearing. When I leave at seven p.m., I worry that he might be violent and get out of bed and attack the other patients. I wonder what his wife must have had to put up with at home. I wonder where his family is and why no one has been to see him. Later, I find out that he has been transferred from a country hospital some four hours away.

The next morning, he is still in the bed and still trying to get out. I notice a restraining garment on the shelf next to the bed.

There is a young male nurse on guard duty and he is clearly becoming frustrated. 'If you keep trying to get out of bed, I'm going to have to restrain you,' he warns.

'Don't put that back on me,' pleads the man, but his restlessness persists and soon the nurse is tying him to the bed.

Later, he is given a sedative and is resting quietly when his brother arrives. The change in him is immediate. With his brother by his side, the restraints are removed and he is able to sit up in bed and have a meal. I hear the brother's soothing words and the calming effect they have. I see their shared tears as they hug. I'd been frightened of this man, of what he might be capable of, and I feel ashamed.

In the bed next to Steve is a seventy-eight-year-old man with Parkinson's. Every day a woman comes to visit him. She brings in his clean washing, fills out his menu and helps him with his lunch. One day, I hear him talking to his wife on the phone. She is in hospital in Sydney recovering from cancer surgery. The daily visitor is a family friend who, in the wife's absence, is taking care of a mate. They'd been on their way to visit the wife in Sydney when he'd collapsed at the train station and been rushed to hospital. The visitor never misses a day. When there is talk of the man going into respite care, she offers to have him at her home. When Steve is discharged, the two friends are chatting together companionably, the patient reclining on his hospital bed and the visitor in the chair beside him.

Steve is home again but he is sicker now. He is so tired he can barely function. He sleeps a lot. Some days, I need to wake him mid-morning to give him his antibiotic. He must stay on this medication for the rest of his life in the hope it will suppress the organism that keeps growing on his scalp. It is a huge tablet and he has trouble swallowing it. To add to my concerns, it needs to be taken twice a day on an empty stomach without dairy products. My attempts to get him to take the antibiotic are often fruitless. In desperation, I resort to crushing the tablet and mixing it with juice, then spoon-feeding it to him. I worry that he isn't getting the full dose every time, because he often spits it out.

The antibiotic also interacts with his antipsychotic medication. The finely balanced regime of drug-taking is teetering as this new interloper disturbs the equilibrium. I am teetering too. I am overwhelmed by the responsibility of Steve's care and the demands it places on me.

One afternoon, when Steve has trouble swallowing his Parkinson's medication, I throw a glass of water over him and then smash the glass into floor. I run from the house, sobbing, to my neighbour. She has witnessed my struggle over the years and somehow knows the right words to give me comfort on this bleak, grey winter's day. We talk until I'm calmer and can once again face Steve. But I know that my days as his carer are now numbered.

*

July 2013. Sometimes I scream – shrill, ear-piercing shrieks that make Steve leave the room and cause the dog to start barking. I shake, I throw things, I sob. I barely recognise the sounds coming from my throat.

*

Years ago, before Parkinson's, and when the winter winds blew, Steve would light the fire on Saturday nights. When we bought our house in 1985, the open fireplace was one feature that attracted us and we imagined spending warm, cosy nights by its side. We soon discovered that most of the heat went up the chimney, that while it warmed our fronts, our backs stayed cold and that the room never heated up sufficiently. We eventually put a combustion heater in the fireplace cavity and covered the gaping arch with a charcoal grey fascia. The stove heated the room more efficiently, though not the whole house as we'd hoped.

Saturdays were busy when the girls were young. I taught ballet in the mornings and, during winter, our daughters played netball. Steve and I never missed a game. The cold winds buffeted the netball courts as we huddled in coats and scarves, eating sausage rolls. Then we hurried back to the warmth of cars to thaw out on the way home.

I would start chopping vegetables for the chicken soup while Steve went out to the woodpile. He'd split the logs, collect the kindling, and then carry it all indoors. Before long, the fire would be blazing, dancing orange flames that licked the roof and glass door of the heater, and we'd be eating big bowls of soup with crusty bread. Or we'd order pizzas and lay out a checked tablecloth on the floor and have a picnic in front of the fire. Later, I'd sit on the carpet and Steve would lie outstretched, his head on my lap as we all watched a movie together.

We pulled up the carpet four years ago. The polished floorboards are too hard to sit on but Steve can't get down onto the floor anyway. We don't light the fire any more. There are plenty of logs on the wood pile but I'm not strong enough to split them. The last time I tried to light the fire, the wood never ignited. The logs were too big and there was not enough kindling. Instead, I sat on the timber floor screwing up sheets of newspaper and filling the cavity of the heater. Every lit match started the paper burning, but each ball of paper combusted then collapsed into the ashes, bringing my carefully constructed kindling down with it. Smoke billowed out into the cold room and I closed the glass door forever.

Now when the winter chill hits, I press the button on the gas heater and the room is warm in minutes. Steve sits in his chair and I curl up on the comfy lounge. Before long, he dozes off and I turn the pages of my book until my eyes grow heavy and I crawl into my bed.

*

The old lady sits in a wheelchair in the foyer. Her ginger hair is permed, her skin is pale and wrinkled. Her hands are clasped together on the crocheted rug that covers her lap.

'Would you like a cup of tea?' I hear an aide ask.

The woman shakes her head. She is happy to just sit, to look out at the world beyond the glass doors of the facility she calls home.

I look around the foyer. The decor is simple but stylish, suggestive of a recent refurbishment. It's a light area with potted palms in corners, easy chairs against walls and a tweed carpet in shades of beige and brown. There are three offices that open off the foyer and two closed double doors, one that says ZONE 1 and another that says ZONE 2.

Sally and I are at the aged care facility to speak with the manager about Steve's condition and the possibility of him needing residential care. I can't believe I'm sitting here, making plans for his future. I've been struggling. The medication regime has changed, hallucinations dominate, and simple tasks are even less achievable. I have to watch he doesn't turn on the hot water tap when he washes his hands. I have to convince him there are no holes in the floorboards when he obsesses about them. I have to make sure dinner is on time or he becomes agitated. I have to try to get him to swallow his medication. His mobility is also less reliable, his balance more precarious. I worry about him on our stairs. He is no longer safe in our home. The doctor says he may still be recovering from surgery but I worry that the changes may be due to a permanent deterioration.

We do a quick tour of the various wards. We walk down long corridors and I glance into bedrooms where white-haired residents are sleeping or sitting in their chairs. Some are ready for lunch, bibs on, waiting patiently at their tables. We enter the secure dementia ward. It's a dark and somewhat cold area. We've already determined that Steve needs to be in a secure section – his sense of direction is still strong and I fear he would just walk out the front door and try to head for home otherwise. But it is hard to imagine Steve in this place and even harder to imagine me visiting him here.

*

To my relief, the doctor puts Steve on a different antibiotic, one tablet a day with no food restrictions. I hide the tablet in a spoonful of ice cream.

*

August 2013. I bump into one of Steve's colleagues from work. She is a retired schoolteacher, a warm, lovely lady whom we haven't seen for several years. She asks me how Steve is and I tell her that he is deteriorating. Then I say how nice it is to see her and that we don't see many of the other teachers any more. She nods and explains that people find it too hard to have a conversation with Steve now.

I bristle at her response. I want compassion and understanding from friends; I expect empathy and support. I want to tell her how hard the past twelve years have been. But Steve's condition is confronting and perhaps I'm being unreasonable. I wonder what my own reaction would be if I hadn't experienced serious illness so intimately.

*

I lash out at Steve, pummelling his chest with my fists. He wards me off his arms raised in self-defence. Then he moves away from me, to the front door, looking for a way out.

*

I have been painting the house, room by room. I choose shades of beige, calm restful colours. I can't bear the bright yellow and blue of Katie's teenage bedroom or the lime green in Sally's old room, so I cover the walls in neutral hues. The old timber kitchen has been renovated and gleams in glossy white – clean, light and fresh. I've replaced the old blue-checked cane furniture in the family room with a contemporary navy sofa. Carpets have been pulled up and timber floors polished. A new modern brown lounge suite is on order to replace the worn, cracked navy blue leather suite in the living room. The home renovation has happened gradually over several years. I cannot bear clutter, so the decor is more minimal now. The house is empty of children, so it stays neater and cleaner. I long for simplicity amid the turmoil.

Steve's bedroom remains untouched. I hate the deep gold walls, the cream built-ins, the lace curtains, the cream quilt cover, the wrought-iron bed. I can't wait to replace the stained carpet, paint the walls and built-ins, install new window coverings and buy a new bed. The old mattress is soiled and needs tossing. One day, I want to remove every trace of these difficult years from this room. I want to forget the struggle my husband endures every time he gets in and out of bed. I want to forget the incontinence products and wet sheets. Our bedroom, once a site for talking and loving, now has too many unpleasant associations, too many disturbing images.

Increasingly, I consider an existence without my husband. I begin preparing for the time when Steve moves into care and then feel disloyal. How can I make this heartbreaking decision? In my distress, I turn to memoir and read *A Three Dog Life: A Memoir* by Abigail Thomas. Thomas writes about her decision to have her husband Rich placed in a locked facility following a traumatic head injury and the guilt she suffers as a result. 'What kind of woman was I? What about my wedding vows? Who was I that keeping hold of my own life was more important than taking care of my husband?' Rich suffers from rages, aggression, paranoia and psychosis, and clearly requires professional care, but Thomas is overcome with shame and remorse. 'What standard do we women hold ourselves to?' she asks.

My standard is high. I don't give up easily. I want Steve to have the best quality of life possible for a man in his condition. I can still care for him but it comes at a price. Joel Havemann, author of *A Life Shaken: My Encounter with Parkinson's Disease*, fears for a future in which he relies on loved ones to stay functioning. His family have promised him they won't put him into an institution but he hopes they will reconsider. 'I don't want any of my family to sacrifice their best years looking after me in my worst,' he says.

What would Steve want for me now? The old Steve would have said, 'Don't worry about me. You go and have fun.' But what would my life be like when my days are no longer measured by the demands of full-time care? How would I cope on my own? How could I deal with the guilt of leaving strangers to look after Steve?

The freedom to pursue my own interests beckons invitingly. The relief of having someone else tending Steve's needs is appealing. But I have also adapted to my role as carer, to the routine and familiarity of looking after Steve. It is difficult to imagine any other way of life.

*

September 2013. Steve is missing. I search for him day after day for two weeks. I look for him in the house, under the bed, in the garage, in the vacant block at the end of our street. I weep daily. I cannot sleep. Then I find him. He is in a lake covered with flowers. He floats under a layer of blossoms – camellias, roses, carnations. They form a carpet in shades of red, pink and white. He is face down. He is dead.

I wake up with a start and the dream recedes. It is early, before six, and today I am taking Steve to an aged care facility for two weeks' respite. His bag is packed and I've told him he's going into hospital to have his medication adjusted. When he wakes, I give him his tablets and breakfast, but I can't eat. His admission goes smoothly. He walks in with me obediently, trustingly. He's settled in his room when I leave and believes my assurance that I will be back.

I return at six p.m. to meet the GP who will chart his medications. I see Steve standing in the dining area flanked by two nurses. They are trying to understand what he wants but he can't make his request understood. Then he sees me and relief floods his face. His bottom lip quivers and I feel as though I have abandoned him. We sit together then until his eyes grow heavy and I put him to bed.

Within days, I see Steve deteriorate. His confusion increases. He quickly suffers daytime incontinence. His appetite is poor (or is it the food?) and he loses more weight. I notice the clothes hanging from his lanky frame. His grasp on reality becomes more tenuous. I become acutely aware of how sick Steve is now. Perhaps it is seeing him in this environment that brings his condition into sharp relief. A new layer of grief envelops me. Every day, I resist the urge to bring him home.

My girls beg me to stick it out. 'Dad will be okay,' they say. 'You need a rest.'

The rhythm of my day changes while Steve is in care. I wake early and think of him waking in a strange bed with strangers looking after him. I need to get out of my own bed quickly or the negative aspects of this admission overwhelm me. Then I try to occupy the hours before I visit him. I enjoy a new sense of freedom as I go about my day but a voice inside my head reminds me that this is at Steve's expense. The nursing unit manager asks me whether I'm going to be 'one of those people who visit every day'. I feel he is judging me, so I delay visits till later in the day when I know he's finished work. I do visit every day. It's the only way I can reassure myself that Steve is surviving this ordeal. Despite my concerns, however, he seems settled and doesn't ask to come home.

Towards the end of the second week, I travel to Merriwa to have an overnight stay with our friend, Jill. It is a two-and-a-half-hour trip, and not long after I arrive, I receive a phone call. Steve has fallen and hit his head. The nurse assures me that he's fine but I get back in the car and drive home. The landscape flies by. If I hadn't placed him in care, he wouldn't have fallen. I've been selfish. The self-recriminations continue unabated until I arrive at the nursing home and find Steve sitting in his chair ready for dinner. He suffers no ill effects from the fall but I check his head carefully for any sign of injury. I worry about the deep brain stimulators and the result of the impact, but he appears unharmed.

One night, Steve wakes and sits on the edge of the bed. The nurse finds him putting his shoes on, getting ready to go home.

My own nights are unsettled. I dream vivid dreams – of scalp infections, of death, of trips alone to exotic countries where I frantically search for Steve.

On the second last day of respite, Sally and Katie come with me to visit their father. Steve is eating when we arrive and he doesn't lift his head or acknowledge us.

Katie bends over to say hello but he doesn't respond. 'He doesn't even know I'm here,' she says softly.

I hear the hurt in her voice and see her eyes fill, but she turns away quickly. Later, we are all sitting together in a small visitor's room, a sparsely furnished space with four chairs, a table and a TV on the wall. The girls and I are chatting when Steve suddenly gets up out of his chair, walks over to Katie and pulls her up from her seat. He takes her in his arms and they begin to dance, a slow *pas de deux* between father and daughter. Katie nestles her head in her father's neck and he puts his arm protectively around her back. It is a natural and instinctive movement that transcends the limitations of his illness. We all wipe away our tears.

*

October 2013. Small children stare at my husband. They do it openly and unselfconsciously. Sometimes, I see fear in their eyes as they clutch their parents' hands. I always smile to reassure them but I see the uncertainty and suspicion in their honest faces. I'm sad that they're frightened of Steve. He loves little kids and they used to love him.

Adults are more subtle. They look away or glance at me sympathetically. Perhaps they've had their own experience with a sick loved one. Sometimes, people are too self-absorbed to even notice. But Steve definitely doesn't look 'right' and people do stare sometimes. I brush aside my discomfort now. I don't worry if the shape of his incontinence pants is visible through his tracksuit. I don't worry if he has food stains on the front of his shirt. I dab his mouth with a tissue to stem the drooling. I hold his hand so he doesn't wander off. I'm no longer embarrassed by his awful table manners.

*

I receive an offer of a bed in an aged care facility and I briefly consider accepting. I explain to Steve that I can't go on looking after him, that he needs professional care. He tells me he will go and live with his brother instead. I don't remind him that his brother died six years ago.

*

November 2013. Steve stands up from his chair and hands me his breakfast plate. I look at the toast crumbs on the plate, sticky with the remnants of honey and butter. I take it into the kitchen, a few steps away from Steve, then walk back into the lounge room, where he stands in his warm blue dressing gown.

I see a look of bewilderment on his face and we both know what will happen next. He falls backwards, like a tree felled in the forest, and hits the floor with a loud THWACK. In that moment, when I knew he would fall, I reached out to him. But the distance was too great and I couldn't have stopped him anyway.

His six-foot frame lands heavily, the polished floorboards unforgiving. The fall shocks him and I hear a loud aaah as the air rushes from his lungs. I cry out too. He has landed in a reclining position on his back, his buttocks and back taking the full brunt of the impact. His head doesn't hit the floor and I am grateful that the brain stimulators are safe.

I rush to him, expecting a serious injury but he appears unscathed, just shaken and winded. Slowly, I help him roll over onto his hands and knees and he is able to push up on the edge of the chair and get to his feet. I quickly help him sit down.

'Does it hurt anywhere?' I ask, but he shakes his head.

He looks dazed but I don't know if this is from the fall or just part of his usual morning fug. I sit quietly too, as I gather my thoughts and recover from the shock.

We are still sitting when the care worker comes to shower Steve thirty minutes later. I tell her that Steve has fallen and we decide to forgo the shower this morning. Before long, I feel my eyes fill and the carer offers some practical advice. She suggests some extra in-home help. She says the shower door can be taken off and we can wheel Steve in for his morning showers now that his mobility is so variable.

I cannot bear the thought of more people coming into my home. I don't want to put Steve in a wheeled shower chair. I don't want to make adjustments to our home to cater for his illness. I don't want to admit that he is getting worse. I don't want a sick husband.

In the afternoon, when another carer comes to provide respite, I escape for two hours. I warn her that Steve has fallen and to keep an eye on him. When I return, she tells me she has rung the coordinator to tell him about the fall. I am short with her, annoyed that she has reported this incident. I remind her that he didn't fall while in her care. She sees I am upset, gathers her belongings and quickly leaves.

Days later, I am still haunted by the sound of Steve falling onto the hard floor.

*

Steve mistakes his recliner chair for the toilet. I see a hot steaming mass on the navy blue leather seat. He has removed his underwear and now I find more deposits on the timber floor. I follow a trail of cow pats up the hallway. They merge with the knots in the wood and I tiptoe carefully, dodging any suspicious spots.

*

December 2013. I see three separate counsellors, all women, all kind and understanding. Two specialise in counselling carers of loved ones with dementia. They listen to my fears, watch me cry and support me. They offer sound advice. I know they are also gently nudging me to consider placing Steve in an aged care facility, a topic that is torturing me. One counsellor points out that I'm like an ant trying to carry a watermelon, such is my load. Another expresses concern for my mental health and well-being. The third assures me I will know when the time is right.

When my aged mother had surgery for a broken hip, she woke up from the anaesthetic confused and frail. She called out for her 'ma' and 'pa', long since dead, and thought the old lady in the bed opposite was my father. Her rehabilitation was slow, painful and difficult and I knew she couldn't go home. My father, whose Alzheimer's had advanced, was in a separate hospital after becoming deranged and aggressive. With both parents in hospital and neither capable of looking after themselves, I met with social workers to discuss their future.

I already knew I couldn't look after my father. We had brought Dad home when Mum was hospitalised for the broken hip and he'd become disorientated. His actions one hot January night had been terrifying and disturbing. Soon after midnight, he had entered our bedroom, a leather belt poised to strike in his hand. He yelled angrily at me. Steve got out of bed and ushered him down the hall away from the bedrooms where the children were sleeping. I stayed huddled under the sheets wondering what was happening to my gentle dad.

Steve sat up with my father all that long night. At some point in the early hours, he took Dad back to the family home to see if that would calm him, but the empty, white weatherboard house stood ghost-like under the full moon and failed to comfort him. At dawn, when he seemed calmer, I got out of bed and gave him some breakfast. Soon, my father started pacing up and down the hallway, peering in our sleeping girls' bedrooms and I became increasingly uneasy. Steve tried to distract him but my father lashed out, kicking him in the shin. Then, when the girls woke, he became verbally aggressive. In despair, I rang a friend and organised to drop the girls at her house. As I drove them to safety, I looked in the rear-vision mirror and saw my eighty-five-year-old father chasing my car up the street. He was hospitalised later that day.

The geriatrician asked whether my mother could come home to live with me. My mother's confusion, she said, was probably related to her surgery and could well ease in the coming weeks and months. I looked at my mother. She was disorientated. She couldn't walk. Even before the broken hip and post-operative problems, she'd had severe osteoporosis and difficulty moving. We had numerous stairs at our house. I had two young children, a husband and a business to run. I couldn't look after her – I couldn't be her nurse.

And so I signed the papers that were put in front of me. My parents would not be going home. They would be placed in a nursing home; the best I could hope for was that I find one where they could be together.

Luckily, they were accepted into an aged care facility in a neighbouring suburb. My brothers and I picked our mother up from hospital and took her to her new home.

She thought we were going out for a Sunday drive and became alarmed when we deposited her into the care of strangers. 'Don't leave me here!' she screamed.

The sound of her anguished cry still echoes twenty years later. My sense of betrayal was profound. However, soon my father was transferred from hospital to the facility as well and they were able to spend his remaining months together.

Contemplating my husband's placement is completely different. My parents were aged and had lived full lives. I came to accept their decline, and when they passed away, I was relieved the suffering was over. But Steve is my life partner and he is young. The decision making is more complex and painful. I secretly hope that the choice is made for me, that an unforeseen crisis will remove any doubt.

*

January 2014. We walk into the day care centre together. It's the first time I've tried leaving Steve at a day facility and I'm apprehensive. Steve is quiet. I haven't told him where we're going or why we're here. I've just said we are going to talk to some nice ladies.

We tried going here once before some years ago. I'd convinced Steve that we were going to a men's group for the day, with lots of interesting activities for him to participate in. We arrived at the same time as the transport bus and watched as the elderly men tottered in on their walkers. 'This looks great,' Steve muttered sarcastically. I had to agree. I couldn't leave my fifty-six-year-old husband here. I turned the car around and we drove home.

The 'nice ladies' meet us in the entry and then take us into a private room to chat. Before long, Steve is ushered into the main room of the facility and I hand spare clothes and medications to the manager. I look around the room. There are two tables set up at one end, a snooker table at the other end, and some comfy chairs against the wall. Grey-haired men are seated around the table. A carer stands at the front and addresses the group. It's trivia time. Trivia would mean nothing to Steve now and I wonder how he'll fit in, but we're here now so I persevere. This is just a trial.

I say goodbye to Steve and drive home. The two hours pass quickly

– I have lunch, go to the shopping centre and then it's time to pick him up. The manager meets me at the door. She tells me Steve was fine but restless, that he kept getting up out of his chair to walk around, that he needed someone with him all the time. He ate some lunch (a hot dog) had a cup of coffee (he doesn't drink coffee) and was taken to the toilet.

Then she tells me they won't be able to take Steve on. 'He needs one on one care and we don't have enough staff,' she says.

I'm confused. Isn't this a dementia care centre? I ask her whether the other men here always sit obediently in their chairs and she nods. She suggests I look for more in-home respite.

I go into the main room to find Steve. He's sitting quietly in a chair and doesn't respond to me at first when I try to help him to stand up. Most of the other men are sitting around the tables playing bingo. Even when he was well, Steve would never have played bingo.

I finally get him to stand and I see that his T-shirt has been tucked into the elasticised waistband of his shorts. I shudder. The carer hands me Steve's medications and spare clothes. Then we walk out into the sunshine and I pull the shirt out of his pants.

*

I am at the supermarket when the checkout lady asks, 'Hubby not with you today?'

I shake my head. 'No, he's at home with a carer.'

The lady gives me a concerned look. 'Do you mind me asking what's wrong with him?'

I tell her and she clucks sympathetically.

'I could see that he was going downhill,' she says.

I rarely take Steve shopping now. It is a confusing experience for him – the noises, the crowds, the extra stimulation. Supermarket shopping is also tiring. It's too far for him to walk up and down the aisles while I look for items. And it's hard for me to concentrate while trying to keep an eye on him. Sometimes, he follows other women and their trolleys and I have to chase him. I can't leave him resting on a seat either in case he gets up and wanders off looking for me.

I usually do my shopping at night now after Steve's tucked up in bed sound asleep. I steal out into the night air and head to the local shops just minutes away. It's often near closing time; fresh vegetables are being packed away ready to store in the cool room, the aisles are lined with boxes as workers restock shelves, the deli counter is being cleaned. I make my purchases quickly; I mustn't be away from Steve for too long. But for a few precious minutes, I feel normal. And free. It's like entering another world.

*

It is hot in the car park. The summer has been dry and warm – unending days of sunshine and heat. I feel beads of perspiration trickling down my back as I try to get Steve out of the car. I'm taking him to the pathology rooms for his monthly blood test, a requirement for his ongoing antipsychotic treatment.

I open the car door and lift Steve's left leg out of the car and onto the asphalt. He is leaning over towards the driver's seat, so I reach in, my arms around his shoulders to straighten him up. He moans slightly as I manoeuvre his body into a more upright position. His eyes are closed against the glare. I swing his left leg out of the car, then his right leg and help turn his body to face the door. I place his right hand on the door handle so he has something to grip and put my arm under his left armpit to help raise him from the seat.

'Can I help you?'

I hear a female voice call out to me. I see a slim young woman in a uniform approach us.

'Do you need a wheelchair?' she asks.

I tell her that once Steve stands, he should be able to walk. 'I just need help getting him out of the car,' I explain, so she leans down and places her arm under his other armpit.

Together, we try to lift him but he cannot stand.

She tells me she works in the X-ray rooms and will get a wheelchair for him. We agree this would be the safest option for him once we get him out of the car. She returns with the chair and we try again. Despite two of us trying to lift him, Steve will not stand. No amount of cajoling helps and we realise that he is resisting our efforts.

The woman says she will go into the pathology rooms and see if the technician will come out to the car to take Steve's blood. I give her his name and she hurries off returning a short time later. The pathology lady cannot leave the rooms unattended.

I thank the woman for her help and tell her I will try again tomorrow.

She looks at me sympathetically. 'Mr Boulton taught me tech drawing in Year 8,' she says.

I feel my eyes well.

'My father just passed away from dementia,' she confides. 'I've just been through this with my mum.' She gives me a hug and when we break apart we both wipe away tears. She offers to help me again, should I need it the next day and then she hurries back into the X-ray rooms.

I drive Steve home. After parking in the driveway, I open the car door for him and he climbs out easily and walks up the front steps.

*

February 2014. Steve has his hair cut. He is booked in for three thirty p.m. and we arrive on time but the hairdresser is running late.

'Won't be long!' she calls out cheerily, but I know it will be a while because the client is sitting in the chair with wet hair still to be cut and blow-dried.

Beside me, Steve becomes restless. I keep reminding him that he's next, that the hairdresser is nearly ready for him. He tries to stand up but the seat is low – to my advantage – and I persuade him to wait a bit longer.

The hairdresser and client are looking at photos on the mobile phone now, laughing and chatting. Then she pulls out the hair straightener and starts working on the girl's long blonde locks. Finally! She's finished! But, no. Now, she starts braiding the girl's hair.

Eventually, the hairdresser ushers Steve over to the chair. He can't work out how to sit in the seat and tries to sit on the bench in front of the mirror. The hairdresser looks at me questioningly but does her best to help me out. She is a kind girl and has cut Steve's hair before, so she knows us. After much persuasion, we manage to turn him round and push the seat under him.

'Just a trim up?' she asks, and I nod.

'Cut a lot off,' I say, 'so I don't have to bring him back in a hurry.'

She laughs then shakes her head. 'I don't know how you do it,' she sympathises.

I pick up a magazine and flip through its glossy pages. When I look up, I see that the hairdresser is having trouble. Steve's head is bent forward and he is leaning over to the side. I put the magazine down and hurry over to her aid. I hold Steve's head up so she can cut. She works quickly and efficiently. When I look down, I see that Steve has dribbled down the front of his cape. The saliva has left big dark patches on the red fabric, sticky with grey curls. I feel I should apologise but don't know what to say. I am beyond words. I just want to get out of here and away from the curious looks of the other customers. On the way home, I vow to look up mobile hairdressers.

*

The bedtime ritual starts early – usually around seven p.m. Steve has little idea of time, so when he wakes after a post-dinner nap, it must seem like the middle of the night. In winter, the nights close in early and the darkness outside confuses his sense of time even more. Sometimes, I encourage him to stay up a little later but, inevitably, he falls asleep in his chair and getting him to bed is more difficult. Mostly, I am happy for him to go to bed early – it allows me some space to relax. I am used to the quiet nights now and don't feel lonely any more.

Every evening, I prepare his medications. I line up his Parkinson's drugs, Stalevo, a tablet he takes every two and a half hours throughout the day, and Sinemet CR, a slow-release tablet that produces the dopamine he needs to enable him to move during the night. I sometimes wonder how necessary the night-time drugs are now, because once he's in bed, he stays in the one position and rarely gets up to use the toilet. I am reluctant to change the regime in case the Parkinson's rigidity sets in and I am unable to get him out of bed in the morning.

Next, I shake the antipsychotic, Clozapine, out of the bottle and put it on the kitchen bench. It is a tiny yellow tablet with a score line down the centre. His dosage has varied over the past two years and sometimes includes half or even quarter tablets. Then I position the small pill on the tablet cutter and try to cut as accurately as possible. Steve is very sensitive to this medication, so I am careful. I look at this tiny tablet and marvel at its power. Without it, Steve would be unbearable. The disturbing hallucinations and delusions would increase and he would become severely agitated. His behaviour would be very difficult to manage. The Clozapine makes him sleep at night and sedates him through the day.

I offer Steve his medication with a big glass of water. Some nights, he has difficulty moving the tablet to the back of the throat so he can swallow. When this happens, the tablet and water pool in his mouth and he eventually has to spit them out in the sink. I stand guard over him until all the tablets are swallowed, and then ask him to open his mouth and show me his tongue so I know they've all gone down. He has difficulty opening his mouth wide.

Once he has successfully swallowed the medication, we move to the bathroom to clean his teeth. He stands at the bathroom door, his hand sliding up and down the architrave. He's looking for the light switch but can't locate it, so I flick on the switch and light floods the room. We move over to the basin. On the vanity are Steve's toothbrush and the toothpaste. There is room for two toothbrushes in the holder but I have hidden mine because otherwise he uses it. Sometimes, he picks up the soap dispenser by mistake and tries to use that. I put toothpaste on the brush and encourage him to clean his teeth. He thoroughly cleans the bottom teeth but has some trouble manoeuvring his hand to clean the top. I have to help but it makes me feel sick pushing the toothbrush into his mouth. It's hard to judge how far back to move the brush. He doesn't like this intervention and I avoid it too.

We move into the bedroom and Steve sits on the edge of the bed. He takes off his socks, shoes and pants. Then I help him remove his top, put on a clean T-shirt and put on his incontinence pull-ups. The bed is ready for him. I have put the sheepskin on his pillow to protect his head and pulled back the sheet and blanket. There is a method for getting him into bed. He sits on the edge of the bed then edges his bottom back before lying down on his right side. I lift his legs onto the bed and then arrange the pillow under his neck. I release his right shoulder and arm so that he is comfortable. Then I pull the covers up to keep him warm, kiss him goodnight and turn off the light. I leave the door ajar so I can hear him during the night.

*

Dear Steve,

I'm writing you this letter because I can no longer have a conversation with you. I miss being able to discuss things with you. I've almost forgotten what that was like. I've almost forgotten what you were like before Parkinson's.

I remember making your lunch and waving you off to work at eight o'clock every morning. You used to ring me when you arrived at school and often rang through the day as well for a quick chat. I remember how we sometimes used to meet for lunch. I would wait for you on the upper level of the shopping centre (near the kebab shop – your favourite) and watch you walk down to meet me. Your curly grey hair was so distinctive you were easy to pick out in a crowd. Your stride was so strong and confident.

I remember the way you used to play with our girls when they were little. You taught them how to ride bikes, how to sink a netball, how to swim. You used to play Marco Polo with all the neighbourhood kids when they turned up for a swim in our pool. I can still hear the children squealing and giggling as you turned on the garden hose and sprayed them.

I remember family holidays together – our annual camping trips, visiting the theme parks on the Gold Coast, taking the girls to Disneyland. You got on every ride with them from the scariest roller coaster to the magical Peter Pan ride. We spent a month in America travelling down the west coast from Seattle to Mexico with a detour out to Las Vegas. You'd been to the US the year before on a G'Day USA trip with school kids and delighted in showing us the sights. I was happy to follow your lead. You were the decision-maker while I often wavered, undecided. You enjoyed social occasions and the company of colleagues and friends while I sat quietly in the background. Our roles are reversed now. I have had to overcome my shyness and speak for both of us. Now, I make all the decisions.

I remember how my ballet students adored you. You loved sharing your skills with them, especially the talented pupils who absorbed every word of advice. Every Christmas concert was a collaborative affair as you helped organise scenery and props while I looked after the choreography and costumes. You often had a leading role: Chinese emperor, jungle chief, the Fonz, King Neptune. In the early years we would perform one of the beautiful *pas de deux* from the classics – *Swan Lake*, *Don Quixote*, *Giselle*. Later, I hung up my pointe shoes and had two babies. When we were forty, we danced together one last time to 'I Know Him So Well' from the musical *Chess*. You wore a black shirt and pants and I, a simple red dress. We have a video of the performance. We still move well together and carry the poise, grace and strength of our earlier dancing days. We look like a couple in love.

But we had problems too. I remember feeling neglected and unloved in the early years of our marriage while you pursued your various interests. I needed more support when the children were young. I became resentful; later, I contemplated leaving. We seemed to have grown apart, gone down diverging paths. Then my parents became ill and I had two households to manage. You held my hand for the next five years as they became sicker and then died.

Just three years later, you became ill. I will never forget the shock of the diagnosis, your deathly white face when the doctor told you, sitting with you at Bar Beach car park while we tried to digest the news, and the crippling fear and grief that have accompanied us ever since. In the early years, you tried to stay positive but, inevitably, you succumbed to the relentless Parkinson's symptoms. The disease has affected every area of our lives.

Now as you become sicker so many things are ending. I can't remember the last time you called me Lindi Lou (your pet name for me), the last time you complimented me, the last time you really enjoyed yourself, the last time you looked happy and content. Of course, I didn't know then that they would be 'last' times. Once, some years after your diagnosis, you told me you could no longer remember what 'normal' felt like. Now, I no longer remember what our 'normal' life was like. We are living a new 'normal' and this is how we will spend the rest of our time together.

Lots of love,
Linda

P.S. I finished this letter last night. This morning, you woke up well. You smiled at me! You responded when I asked you questions. You gave me a hug and patted my back the way you used to. The Steve who's been missing over the past months suddenly reappeared. Just when I'd given up hope, you came back to me and even if it's just for a minute, an hour or a day, it gives me hope that we still have some quality time left together.

Coda

A panoramic view of the lake stretches out before me. This vista of water and sky is spectacular at any time of the day, but is especially beautiful in the early evening, just as the sun is setting. At dusk, the pink and orange tinged billowing clouds are reflected in the glassy expanse of water. When it is calm, two black swans cruise this area. Sometimes, they float, two dark masses coiled near the lapping shores. Their long necks dip down into the dark waters, bright red beaks disappearing before resurfacing to primp and preen. They drift together as the water ebbs and flows beneath them, two graceful birds performing an exquisite *pas de deux*.

*

February 2014. The road to the aged care facility traces the shores of Lake Macquarie. I know the road well, every curve, intersection and merge of traffic. I have been travelling this route to see Steve every day, usually twice a day. I've timed the trip – twelve minutes during off-peak and fifteen when it's busy.

I like looking at the lake as I drive. On bright sunny days, the water is an intense blue. When it is stormy, white caps ruffle the surface and the water is grey and choppy. We have a view of the lake from our home; it was the main attraction when we bought the house. I can almost see the care facility from our house – if I could only see past the curve of the headland and past the trees, I'd be able to see where Steve now lives. Still, I like that when I look out of my kitchen window I can see the same water that Steve sees from his bedroom window.

That first day, the car packed with Steve's belongings, my heart hammering, the drive to his new home passed in a blur. I didn't see the lake that day. I remember arriving, looking for him. The patient transport delivered him twenty minutes later and he was wheeled down to his room, a flurry of nurses following. Steve lay on the bed pale and silent while I was asked about his dietary requirements and medications. I remember a cleaner coming in to mop his bathroom floor, and the tattoo on the nurse's arm. I remember sobbing uncontrollably and Steve rubbing my back, consoling me. I remember him getting up off the bed and taking a few steps and the joy of seeing him on his feet after being bedridden in hospital for two weeks. Later, we walked outside in the garden, the February sunshine warm on our backs.

I was relieved that Steve was out of hospital. He'd been so unwell prior to his admission. The Parkinson's symptoms had intensified and I'd been frightened when he couldn't walk or even stand by himself. How could I look after him on my own if he wasn't mobile? The ambulance had taken him to hospital and over the following days I talked to the doctor, the Parkinson's nurse and the social worker. They warned me that such episodes might keep recurring – more hospitalisations as his condition worsened. Perhaps this was the time to consider residential care, to share the burden of looking after Steve. Plans were put into place and papers were signed. When a bed became available in a nearby facility, I accepted it. At least he would be close to home. At least he would be safe.

The care facility sits at the point of a headland. There is a sharp left turn at the bend in the road and then a steep drive down past the retirement living to Steve's unit. Behind the building, grassy slopes lead down to the waterfront. Large leafy trees provide shade for picnic tables and benches. The view is breathtaking.

Steve's unit is perhaps twenty-five years old. It is large and rambling, catering for the thirty dementia residents who wander its floors. The unit is sparsely furnished in shades of beige and blue with lino floors and cream curtains – the same curtains we have in our own house. The decor is basic, a minimalistic approach. The main lounge room has a large television mounted to the wall. A piano stands against another wall and a grandfather clock in the corner. High-backed chairs line the walls. There are another two living areas, all with views of the lake. In one, a fish tank burbles. Bookshelves line walls. I see photo boards dating back to 2009. Some of the current residents are in those photos and I wonder how long they've been here, living in this environment.

Steve's room contains a bed and several sets of drawers. An old painting of a sailing boat hangs on the wall opposite the bed. Otherwise, the room is bare. Down one end, near the door, is a kitchen sink and cupboard. This was once a self-care unit. Opposite the sink is a door leading into a bathroom. On close inspection, I see the ingrained grime and mould on the white-tiled floor and walls, the tarnished mirror and the warped interior of the bathroom cupboard. I grimace but Steve won't care – he'd be happy living in a tent. I swallow my disapproval. At least he has a private room and en suite, a haven away from the other residents.

Steve doesn't question the move on that first day. He doesn't ask to come home – that will come later. He accepts his new surroundings. Perhaps, like me, he is just happy to be free of the restrictions of his recent hospital stay, where he'd been confined to bed. When I'd questioned the hospital staff, I'd been told that Steve could no longer weight-bear or walk. My pleas for an assessment by a physiotherapist had been ignored. By the end of his stay in hospital, Steve was being hoisted into and out of bed. To my horror, the handover report to the care facility stated that he was now permanently bedridden.

On that first day, I am nervous when I ask the nurse about rules for patients and their families.

She looks at me sympathetically and reassures me. 'We're not as regimented as a hospital,' she says. 'We're flexible here. This is Steve's home now.'

When Steve finally falls into bed at the end of that long, exhausting day, I drive home thinking maybe everything will be all right.

*

March 2014. The early weeks after Steve's placement pass in a blur of mixed emotions – relief that I'm no longer faced with the daily challenges of full-time care, but also great sadness over our separation and new living arrangements. I still want to be Steve's primary caregiver but the demands are too high. Does he feel abandoned? Have I failed him? I can't bear the thought of handing Steve over to strangers and relinquishing the role I now so strongly identify with. Our co-dependency, as husband and wife and patient and caregiver, has evolved over many years together and is now threatened by our separation. I am distraught and weep over this latest loss until a friend reminds me I will always be Steve's carer, that this role won't stop because he is in the facility, and that he needs me now more than ever.

Steve's medications, once such an arduous task, are now managed by the nursing staff. I find surrendering this duty the most difficult. Due to regulations, there is no flexibility with his medications, no opportunity to change the timing or dosage of his tablets when needed. I worry constantly that the infection on his scalp will resurface. This could potentially be a life or death situation – if the infection comes back and the DBS leads are removed, he will suffer the full consequences of his Parkinson's and, probably, would not survive. I obsessively check that Steve is swallowing his daily antibiotic, often timing my visits to coincide with medication time. I drill the nurses to check that he has swallowed the drug – occasionally, he pools the tablet in his mouth or spits it out when the nurse's back is turned. Sometimes, I find the distinctive orange antibiotic half-dissolved on the floor, under the dining chair or in his bathroom, for example. Because I'm responsible for purchasing this specialised medication from the hospital pharmacy, I know when a new prescription is due and whether he's missed any doses. I struggle to control my anxiety over the pills and try to hide my paranoia. The nurses are incredibly patient with me.

After Steve has been in care for a few weeks, the unexpected happens: he improves. He starts walking better, eating better, becomes more alert and gains weight. I look for reasons. Is the care better than I could provide? What did I do wrong? What was I missing?

Guilt overwhelms me. Steve had been so ill I thought the disease had progressed to the next stage and that I wouldn't be able to cope.

Now I'm filled with doubts about my decision to place him into care. I confess my angst to the nursing staff and the medical professionals looking after him. They try to reassure me but I'm not convinced.

Soon after Steve goes into care, his father is also admitted. The old man has been in hospital for three months after badly lacerating his hand in an accident and then being diagnosed with cancer. He is old and frail and determined to die. Collin occupies the room opposite Steve and barks at anyone who enters. He refuses to eat and within weeks he passes away. Steve says nothing. He sees his father's lifeless body and attends the funeral. There are no tears. Soon, another elderly man moves into the room and Steve doesn't mention his father again.

*

Morning. I open my eyes. A small sliver of light peaks through from behind the curtain and I can tell from its rosy hue that today will be sunny. A chorus of morning birds penetrates the silence. I am alone, the house quiet.

The dream I have woken from is still vivid. A friend has been murdered and her husband is the assassin. I can still feel the distress of this double tragedy. As my eyes adjust to the lightening room, the dream recedes and I remember Steve isn't here. The reality washes over me, raw and unabated.

It takes effort to drag myself out of bed. I walk past Steve's bedroom, the bed empty. There is a space in the living room where his chair used to stand. The morning ritual, once so onerous, no longer occurs. I turn on the television, anxious to break the silence. Then I collapse onto the lounge until I can face the day.

Steve wakes alone, too. A nurse brings him his first medication for the day at eight a.m. He often goes back to sleep then, and the staff get him up when he's ready. Sometimes, he wakes early and gets himself out of bed. His bed alarm goes off and sings 'Somewhere Over the Rainbow' until someone comes to turn it off and attend to him. I like that he doesn't have to be up at a certain time. What is there to get up for?

He is showered every second day. I wish it was every day but showering thirty residents every day would be impossible. On the off days, Steve sometimes looks slightly unkempt – hair messy, grey stubble on chin, greasy skin. His oily skin is a constant problem, an ongoing Parkinson's symptom; the layer of oil coating his skin is often mistaken for sweat. His scalp is flaky too, a form of dermatitis. I'm constantly brushing flakes from his skin and clothes. I wonder if he gets annoyed with my fussing. Steve no longer cares much about his appearance. Now, he sometimes refuses a shave or wash.

At home, I manage a small breakfast and then dress. There are jobs that need doing – last night's dishes, some washing, perhaps some vacuuming. But the house stays tidy and clean now that I am on my own and I only need to wash clothes once a week. If the weather is fine, I take Archie for a walk. We climb our steep street and turn onto the ridge. It's a well-worn path that we walk. From the top of the hill, I can look out across the lake and see the roof of the care facility emerging from the trees. Steve's unit has a white roof so it's easy to pick out amongst the other buildings. I pause. Is he up yet? Does he wonder every morning where he is? Is he missing me?

Lunch. The nurse places a clothes protector over Steve's head. I try to see the logic in this but hate to see my husband wearing a bib. Steve usually takes it off anyway, annoyed by it, and I am secretly pleased that he still has enough sense of himself to reject this institutionalised practice. Mealtimes punctuate the day and fill in time. I help Steve, chopping his food and encouraging him to eat. My own lunch, a rushed cheese sandwich, will be eaten later in the car when we go for our daily drive.

When I drive into the car park, I see his stooped figure standing at the gate waiting for me. Sometimes, I see him pacing the garden. I remember my father doing the same thing when he was admitted to a psychiatric hospital for his dementia twenty years ago. I drove into the hospital grounds and saw my dad, his silver head in his hands, as he sat on a garden bench. Then he stood and walked over to the fence, his hands gripping the black bars that imprisoned him. I didn't understand dementia then and had been frightened when he'd become violent towards me. I thought his aggression was permanent and I'd left him to the care of strangers in unfamiliar surroundings. I was angry with him and hadn't visited for days. How confused and anxious he must have been. Later, when we'd sat together in a sterile dining room with shiny lino floors, white walls and fluorescent lighting, he'd said sorry and we'd both cried.

It takes a while for Steve to register my arrival but he's always relieved to see me. I join him in the pacing or we sit outside in the sun. It's hard to find something to talk about. Sometimes, he asks me where I've been.

He's always anxious to go out and is often impatient. 'Are we going?' he'll say as soon as his meal is finished.

I take him for a drive most days. We tour around the lakeside suburbs or into Newcastle for a scenic drive around the beaches. We go for short walks and ice creams. Sometimes, we visit friends. I avoid driving near our own suburb, though he often points towards home as we drive through neighbouring areas. His sense of direction is still strong and I try to distract him. He asks me where we're going and I flounder for excuses. When we drive through the entrance to the facility, I hear Steve mutter under his breath. Sometimes, he swears. I continue down the winding drive to his unit. Steve gets out of the car compliantly and I lead him back in through the gate.

Evening. I arrive at five p.m. to help Steve with his meal. Some residents are sitting at their tables, others are on the move, barely taking the time to eat. Occasionally, it is Steve who is restless. The snack-type food in the evenings is often inadequate or unappetising and I take Steve out in the car to McDonald's. We go early, before it gets busy, and Steve eats his meal quickly. This is not a fine dining experience. We don't converse. He enjoys his hamburger and fries and for a few minutes life feels more normal.

When we return, I punch the code into the keypad on the security gate. At night, when the day is winding down, we go into his bedroom, close the door and pretend we are in the lounge room at home. I turn on the television, pull up a chair and sit with Steve until he is ready for bed. He sits in his blue recliner chair, brought from home. Sometimes, he dozes while waiting for the nurse to bring him his final medications for the day. At other times, he is wide awake and agitated. Other residents often enter his room by mistake, confused about where they are staying for the night. Often, they worry they have no money to pay for their bed and food.

I like to help the nurses put Steve to bed. I like to position the pillows for comfort, to draw the blankets up over his body and to kiss him goodnight. I need to know that he is comfortable. It takes ages for me to leave. I turn off the TV, tidy the room, gather my things, and still I go back for one last kiss. Parting is excruciating.

Eventually, I turn off the lights and close the door. Sometimes, he is already asleep, but often his eyes follow me to the door. I walk quickly to the car. As I leave the car park, I drive past his bedroom and imagine him lying there on his narrow hospital bed. Then I follow the winding road up the hill, turn onto the main road and head for home.

My house is dark and unwelcoming. I switch on lights, the TV, draw the curtains, feed the dog. Then I open the fridge, looking for something easy to cook. Tonight I settle for scrambled eggs on toast and eat alone. It is eight p.m. – only a couple of hours until bedtime.

*

April 2014. One evening, when I'm driving Steve back to the facility from an outing, he mumbles something. I can't catch what he says and ask him to repeat himself.

'Make sure you enjoy yourself,' he says clearly.

But I can't enjoy myself. A counsellor asks me if I'm punishing myself. Sometimes, Steve asks to come home and I long to bring him home. But then a small hard part of my heart tells me 'NO!' His condition is too much for one person to handle.

I become ill for the first time in years and it takes weeks to recover. At night when I lie in bed, I put the spare pillow close to my back. I miss Steve's body pressed against me, hugging me in the night. I yearn for my mother's comfort. In my anxiety, I turn to Sally and she becomes the parent and I the child.

For the first time in my life, I am living alone. No parents, no husband, no children. I am in limbo – married in name but without a husband.

*

Centrelink says I am no longer Steve's carer and the carer payments stop. Centrelink says I can now apply for Newstart unemployment benefits.

*

May 2014. Katie and her fiancé, Mat, move in with me. They are between houses, preparing for a wedding and starting new jobs. They breathe life back into me and the house becomes a home again.

*

June 2014. Steve has an appointment with the neurologist. My brother gives us a lift to the hospital appointment so I don't have to find a parking spot. He drops us off at the door and we make our way through the corridors to the clinic.

There are patients already waiting: an elderly woman leafing through a magazine, an adult cerebral palsy patient with his elderly parents, a father in a wheelchair bouncing his toddler on his knee. We take our place sitting at the end of a row of seats in the centre of the room. Before long, Steve starts leaning over sideways. I sit on his left, supporting his weight with my body. He begins dribbling and I grab a handful of tissues from my bag as the saliva drips onto my jeans.

The doctor is running late and Steve becomes restless. I see a car magazine in a pile of papers and offer it to him, but it fails to distract him despite his continued obsession with cars. He stands and tries to put his tissue in the elderly woman's walker. I apologise to the woman and she smiles kindly, but I'm embarrassed. Steve is up and down out of his chair, wanting to leave. He doesn't understand why we are here and doesn't want to cooperate. I can't wait to take him back to the facility.

*

The care staff find Steve on his hands and knees in a wardrobe.

*

'One, two, three, four, five, six, seven, eight, nine, ten.' An elderly resident in the care facility is constantly counting. 'Thirty-one, thirty-two, thirty-three, thirty-four, thirty-six, forty.' If she's not counting, she's singing. The same song, over and over, again. 'Seventy-six, seventy-seven, seventy-eight, seventy-nine, eighty.' She is a wizened little woman, a tiny scrap of humanity attached to a wheelchair. 'Ninety-three, ninety-four, ninety-five, ninety-nine, a hundred.' Her husband visits her every day. Someone told me she has eight children. 'Ten, nine, eight, seven, six, five, four, three, two, one, BLAST OFF!'

*

She is an attractive middle-aged woman with shoulder-length auburn hair. Her breasts are full, her stomach flat, her buttocks rounded, her legs shapely. Her body is curvaceous, desirable, womanly. She wears modern clothes – pretty florals or stylish stripes. Sometimes, she completes her outfits with odd shoes, one pink and one grey, or a pair of smart leather boots even if the day is hot. Occasionally, the nurse braids her hair in a glamorous style, but usually her hair is wild and untidy, her look unkempt.

She glides down the corridors clutching a shoe (or toothbrush, or jacket... Sometimes she smiles, sometimes she stares vacantly ahead, and sometimes her look is menacing. She is fifty-eight years old. She was working as a nurse just two years ago.

One day, when I am feeling tired and overwhelmed, I dissolve into tears while visiting Steve.

She sees my distress and asks, 'Are you okay?'

*

August 2014. I am driving home from visiting Steve at the care facility. It is seven thirty, a winter night, and it is raining. I turn onto the dual carriageway, where the amber street lights cast an orange glow over the wet, shiny road. Houses and trees flash past. Cars overtake me. I squint against the bright headlights of a car travelling in the opposite direction.

I drive slowly and an overwhelming weariness settles upon me. I am tired of the guilt, grief and pain of being separated from Steve. How easy it would be to just let the car drift. The urge to do so is suddenly irresistible and I grip the steering wheel, focusing on the road in front of me. The rain is falling harder now and the wipers struggle to keep up. The concrete barrier separating the lanes looms closely. I think about our daughters; I think about Steve. Then I turn off the main road, into our street and the safety of home.

*

October 2014. I place the birthday cake in front of Steve. There are six candles on the cake – an abbreviation of his sixty years. We gather around: wife, daughters, brother, sister and nieces. After I light the candles, we sing happy birthday. We are in a restaurant and other diners look up from their meals at the familiar strains.

'Blow the candles out,' I whisper, but Steve sits staring at the cake.

Everyone waits expectantly, silently willing him to perform this simple task.

I'm anxious to celebrate this special occasion. A decade ago, when we both turned fifty, I organised a party at a local golf club. I'd almost cancelled the planned celebration after Steve had been hospitalised for a psychosis just two months earlier. We were both still fragile from that event, tentatively recovering our relationship. But the birthday party had been a happy occasion shared with family and friends.

Ten years later, our birthdays will be celebrated separately. I pick Steve up from the facility and take him to a local restaurant for his favourite, fish and chips. He becomes restless after the meal but I persuade him to stay seated, reminding him we have cake. Now, I urge him again to blow out the candles and still no response. An awkward silence ensues, so I gently blow, extinguishing the flames. Everyone cheers and Steve manages a smile. Perhaps he does realise it's his birthday after all.

Steve usually enjoys cake but he struggles today. The cream-filled sponge is messy and globs of jam and cream drop off the spoon onto his lap. I eat my piece of cake quickly, one eye on Steve. I wipe his fingers and mouth and then he is on his feet, ready to go. He wanders off as I say a hasty goodbye to our family and then I run to catch up with him before he disappears through the front door.

*

November 2014. I take Steve home for a visit. He has been in the care facility for nine months and I have been too frightened to bring him home. I worry that seeing his house again will be too traumatic and that he'll refuse to go back to the facility. Now, I decide to risk it. I want to spend time with him at home and I need to gauge his reaction to his home environment.

It's a Sunday afternoon and Katie is at home. I park the car in the drive and Steve climbs confidently up the front steps. He trips and stumbles at the front door, but I hold him up and guide him through. He walks into the family room and sits down to take off his socks and shoes, an old habit. We let Archie in and Katie leads him over to Steve for a pat. The dog jumps up at him and Steve fends him off, overcome by his energy and boisterousness.

The visit ends abruptly when Steve stands and walks over to the kitchen bench. He picks up my spectacles case and a biro and moves into the hallway where he pauses. He looks left towards the bedrooms and right towards the living room, then walks to the front door. I suggest going out for an ice cream and he happily walks down the front steps and gets into the car.

*

December 2014. I begin renovating the main bedroom. It is ten months since Steve went into care. His bed, stripped bare, is still in the room, his collared shirts and long pants still hang in the wardrobe. His underwear is still folded neatly in the drawer. Steve's clothes now consist of elasticised shorts, trackpants, T-shirts and windcheaters. The intricacies of shirt buttons and zippers are beyond him and his underpants are now redundant.

The room needs to be painted and new carpet laid. Mat, Katie's fiancé, paints the walls and ceiling for me during his holidays. I choose the same neutral colour scheme used in the spare bedrooms. The wardrobes, coated in enamel paint, need to be sanded and painted and new handles attached to the doors and drawers. I struggle removing the old knobs; they seem stuck and I'm worried about damaging the timberwork. I'm reluctant to ask for help but eventually call a neighbour. He pops out the handles easily and I feel incompetent. When I go to the hardware shop, I can't find suitable handles. I don't like the selection so I go online to look for other options, but am overwhelmed by the choices.

I scour carpet shops looking for the right colour and price range. I bring home various samples and lay them side by side on the floor. I'm not happy with any of them – they're too light, too dark, too shaggy, or too flat. The neutral shades, so attractive in the store, are mushroom pink on my bedroom floor. When I finally decide on the carpet, the salesman expresses concern about the carpet fitting under the existing built-in cupboard doors.

I sit on the bedroom floor in tears. My husband, a woodwork teacher, would have been able to fix all these problems. He would have sanded and painted the cupboards, chosen new door handles, and helped make a decision on the carpet. He would have shaved off the bottom of the doors if necessary to make the carpet fit. He would have taken care of everything.

*

March 2015. A black and white photo. A man and woman dancing. In the background, in the top right-hand corner, a blinding spotlight sends its rays over the man's shoulder, outlining the curve of his back and his snowy white hair. He is wearing a dark suit and light shirt unbuttoned at the collar. A corsage is pinned to the lapel of his jacket. His right arm is firmly around his daughter's waist, his hand settling against the pale lace bodice of her wedding gown. His gold signet ring with its black border is clearly visible. The bride clasps his hand in hers. The grip is secure, and reassuring, the bond between father and daughter unmistakeable.

Pure joy creases Steve's face. He is laughing, the skin pulled tight against his cheekbones. Katie smiles, her eyes drawn to her father. Later, the wedding photographer posts the photo on social media. He writes about our family, of Steve's condition and the problems photographing someone with his disabilities, and of his gratitude at capturing this priceless moment.

Another photo: Steve is on his knee, one arm stretched upwards in a ballet pose, the other positioned firmly on his hip. He has just finished the male solo from the ballet *Don Quixote* and this is the final moment of a complicated series of jumps and turns. The photographer shoots him from behind. The stage light overhead is caught in a prism of colour, a kaleidoscope of rays that shine over his body. His upturned face is bathed in light. Exhilaration oozes from his youthful frame.

*

Steve stands naked before me. His bony shoulders jut out giving his body a rectangular look. The skin hangs from his chest and stomach. It is wrinkled and saggy. He doesn't eat enough to have a paunch now and his flat belly disappears downwards into his nether regions. His hips are prominent, hard structures, still solid and strong. I can feel the ball joints beneath his skin when I tuck him into bed.

His arms hang by his side, pale and freckled. There are dry areas – skin cancers perhaps? – on his forearms. Even his fingers have lost weight. They, too, are naked. I have taken off his wedding and signet rings and have them at home for safe keeping. When he's agitated, he fiddles with the rings, forcing them onto fingers that don't fit, or taking them off and losing them.

His long legs are thin and rangy. I look at the old bruises on his shins. One is the result of a fall off his bike. He'd insisted we'd go for a ride along the cycleway near our home. We'd been standing at the kerb waiting for a break in the traffic, when he'd run impulsively across the busy road and stumbled trying to get his bike up onto the grassy verge. Later, his foot had become caught in the pedals, and he'd fallen again. We'd argued then and I'd refused to let him ride any further. We were a long way from home – too far to walk – so I rang Sally and asked her to pick us up. When I'd taken off his tracksuit pants later that night, I'd seen the deep lacerations on his shin. It had taken two courses of antibiotics and weeks of visits to the doctor's surgery to have the wound dressed before it had finally healed. I asked my neighbour to store the bikes for us and after a while Steve stopped asking about them.

Only his feet look normal. There are a few more spidery veins perhaps, but these are the same feet that slipped into ballet shoes and carried him with such grace and strength. The podiatrist comes to cut his toenails now, a job I hated, and he tells me Steve's feet are in good condition. There are no calluses or bunions.

Steve never wears pyjamas. I help him put a fresh T-shirt over his head. Then I stand before him with the nappy in my hands. During the day, he wears pull-up pants but at night we struggle with a wrap-around affair. I secure the waistband and then pull the nappy up between his legs. I velcro the tabs to the waistband and he lifts each leg slightly to get a more comfortable fit. He doesn't cringe, argue or complain. He looks like a man in his eighties.

*

April 2015. A severe storm lashes the area. Destructive winds fell trees and power lines. Torrential rain floods low-lying areas. The lake rises and parklands and jetties disappear under its muddy waters. It is dark when the storm gains strength. I lie in bed listening to the roar of the gale-force winds and the sheets of rain buffeting the house. I get up periodically to check Archie, who is huddled outside in his kennel. He looks out at me from his snug house seemingly unperturbed by the ruckus, but I have a vision of him being tossed into the air, swept up by a funnel of wind like Dorothy and Toto. At some point in the night, I hear a chainsaw. Later, I move into another bedroom where the noise is less intense. When I look out of the bedroom window, I see the gum trees in the front yard swaying dangerously in the wind.

The full impact of the storm becomes clear the next day. Police and SES warn people to keep off the roads but I drive to see Steve at lunchtime as usual. The trip is uneventful but there is clear evidence of the wild weather – branches littering roads, a houseboat washed up against the shoreline, damaged houses. As I drive along the ridge near the care facility, I see wires dangling from telegraph poles and trees across the road.

A nurse comes out to meet me at the gate when I reach Steve's unit. The power is out and the security pad isn't working. The gate is now secured with a chain and padlock and she jangles keys looking for the right one to let me in. Inside, the residents are sitting at the dining tables. The room is eerily quiet – no television or music playing. The fire doors have closed automatically due to the power outage. The residents are served fish and chips on plastic plates and eat with plastic knives and forks. They drink from plastic cups.

It is a grey day and the dining room is dark and chilly. I worry that Steve is cold, so after lunch I walk him down to his room and put an extra jumper on him. As we walk back up the hallway towards the lounge room, the lights come on. A generator has started working and a wave of relief washes over me. Lights, warmth and the television come on, but within minutes the power goes off again. The nurses are told to turn off the heating and television. These drain the generator. A nurse goes looking for blankets and returns with brightly coloured crocheted rugs to place on elderly knees. The activities officer drags out a game of quoits to occupy the residents.

'Don't come back tonight,' the nurses plead. 'It's not safe to be on the road in the dark,' they warn me.

I heed their advice and spend the evening at home as the wind rises in strength again and the rain pelts down.

The generator is still running intermittently the next day. A serviceman has been called out but is unable to fix the problem. It's not as cold today but the grey skies are depressing and the residents sit glumly in front of a blank television screen. Tonight's meal is lamb's fry and bacon served on plastic plates. The power goes off again several times during dinner and the dining room is dimly lit by the emergency lights. The staff cheer every time the lights come on again. I'm told a maintenance man is sitting out in the weather pressing a button every time the generator turns off so that the facility can have power. I picture him huddled against the elements. The residents are unsettled, confused by the changed circumstances, and are kept in the dining room until an early bedtime beckons. When I get Steve ready for bed, I notice his soft pillow from home is missing. None of the other pillows I find are suitable and I can't raise the bedhead because the power is off. I'm unable to position the new pillows successfully under Steve's neck and he looks uncomfortable. Safe and comfortable in my own bed, it takes me a long time to get to sleep.

The next morning, I make an early visit to the care facility. It's eight thirty, much earlier than the lunchtime time slot I normally adhere to. I find Steve comfortably asleep in his bed, the pillows angled under his head. I sit in his chair in the corner of the room and watch him sleep. He twitches occasionally, jerky movements that overtake his body. Suddenly, his eyes open, startling me. They are clear and blue and stare unblinking at a point somewhere high on the wall behind me. Then, they close again and the twitching resumes. I leave him there sleeping soundly.

The sun is shining as I drive home along the ridge and down the winding road that traces the edge of the lake. The old jetty, submerged by the storm, re-emerges as the lake recedes. A row of pelicans perch on the old timber boards, drying their feathers in the sunlight. The lake laps calmly against the shore.

*

May 2015. We are sitting companionably in Steve's room, he in his comfortable blue leather recliner, me in the pink, upright hospital-style chair. The television drones on in the background. I flick between quiz shows on opposing channels. Someone wins $100,000. The news comes on – a bride-to-be murdered, a woman drives her car into a lake and three children drown. I turn the volume down and read while Steve sits staring at the floor. Twice, he gets up and goes to the bathroom. I follow him, hovering. Perhaps he needs to use the toilet? No. He wanders back into the bedroom and I offer him food. He has eaten sparingly at dinnertime. Maybe he's still hungry. He eats a proffered egg sandwich and half a Kit-Kat. He drops the other half on the floor and I quickly place it in the small blue bin on the bench before he can pick it up and put it in his mouth. I see a small cockroach scurry from under the fridge and disappear beneath a set of drawers.

The curtain is closed against the encroaching darkness of a cool autumn evening. Winter approaches, his second in the care facility, and I dread the colder months with its short days and grey skies. No more after-dinner walks down to the waterfront to escape the confines of the locked facility and its residents. Then the drive home in the dark.

Now, Steve stands up and walks to the door. I ask him where he's going.

'I'm going to wait for my wife,' he tells me.

I stand next to him and ask her name.

'Linda,' he says.

I remind him that I'm his wife, but he gazes down at me disbelievingly. I am unaccountably offended, my devotion redundant and unappreciated.

A nurse interrupts the moment when she comes into his room with his bedtime medications. She helps him clean his teeth and changes his clothes. She replaces his incontinence pad. I curl up on his chair and observe.

*

After we have been on a day outing, I drive into the entrance of the care facility and Steve mutters beside me, 'Where are you putting me this time?'

*

June 2015. Steve punches a resident today. She is an irritable lady who frequently yells abuse at people. She hates men. The nurse tells me the incident will have to be reported. It appears the attack was unprovoked but Steve tells me the woman hit him first. I ask the nurse about the repercussions. I'm frightened they will medicate Steve to sedate him if he does it again but she says nothing will happen for now. I think of another resident, an elderly man who is aggressive with the staff. He is confined to a tub chair now, his face sunken in around his toothless mouth. He is so heavily medicated the staff can barely wake him for meals. In his more alert moments, he strips his clothes off or tries to claw his way out of the chair.

I sit with Steve while he has his lunch. I turn my back away from the staff, hoping my tears fall unnoticed. Steve has been agitated at times but never aggressive. I cannot shake the image of my own father threatening me with a belt in the last months of Alzheimer's. Or of him sitting in the locked geriatric ward of a psychiatric hospital, his body drugged into obedience, his head bowed on his chest. Why do the people I love most in the world have to be so afflicted?

*

August 2015. I go back to ballet. I stand at the *barre*, feet in first position. The music starts and I begin the first exercise – *pliés*. My body remembers. The familiar bending and stretching of limbs, the tightening and flexing of muscles, the movement and music, are as familiar as breathing. I am at an adult ballet class, the first I have attended in over three decades. It feels like coming home.

*

December 2015. The doctor rings early. I am just out of bed, my eyes still blurry with sleep, my voice thick. The pathology results on two skin lesions removed from Steve's shoulder are back and one is a melanoma. I ask which lesion is the cancerous one. Steve had a suspicious-looking freckle removed from the tip of his shoulder and an ulcerated scaly lesion from further back on his shoulder. Surprisingly, it is the latter that has tested positive. The doctor asks for Steve's medical history; he is the GP assigned to the care facility and doesn't know Steve well. He asks whether Steve could undergo a general anaesthetic. He explains that surgery and a skin graft would be involved and a body scan to see if the cancer is spread. I remind him of the deep brain stimulators and pacemaker.

Then he asks me whether Steve would be able to make a decision about having treatment. I look over to Katie, who is getting ready for work. She's sitting quietly on the couch, tears rolling down her cheeks. I tell the doctor Steve is incapable of making such a decision and my mind is racing. Please don't ask me to make this decision. The doctor mutters something about this being 'a hard one'. We both know Steve's poor cognitive state and his impatience over medical procedures. On our last visit to the doctor's surgery, he had paced restlessly in the waiting room like a recalcitrant toddler, refusing to sit still. Then the nurse and I had needed to restrain him while the doctor performed the minor surgeries on his shoulder. Steve had no understanding of why he was there or what the doctor was doing.

The doctor tells me he will consult with a melanoma surgeon and ring me back. I promise to speak to the Parkinson's nurse, who has a thorough knowledge of Steve's condition. When I discuss this latest diagnosis with her, she is sympathetic and concerned. We deliberate over Steve's poor cognitive state and his increasingly frail condition. But do we have the right to determine his quality of life? He is still mobile, he can still eat, he enjoys our daily drives and still recognises the familiar people in his life. We don't want to put Steve through any more trauma.

When the GP rings back two days later, he allays my fears. He has spoken to the specialist and a decision has been made. He tells me if the melanoma returns it will come back to the same area, so the plan is to make a wider incision under local anaesthetic. No hospitalisation, general anaesthetic, skin graft or scan will be required. If Steve had been a young man in good health with his life ahead of him, more aggressive follow-up treatment would have ensued.

The doctor assures me, 'Parkinson's will be the cause of his demise, not melanoma.'

Later, I worry about the diagnosis. I'm unconvinced about the test results. Surely the malignancy refers to the strange-looking freckle on his shoulder not the red spot on his back; it wasn't even a freckle or a mole. Perhaps the doctor mixed up the specimens and the wrong lesion has been identified as melanoma. What if they excise the wrong area? I ask for an appointment with the GP to clarify this. I ask to see the pathology reports. The doctor is patient with me but my paranoia has escalated. I'm sure he thinks I'm unhinged but even I recognise this as a reflection of my ongoing anxiety over Steve's health and my strong feelings of responsibility. I feel we are being punished and that I'm to blame – for not getting the spot checked sooner and for wishing, at times, for Steve to die.

At night, I wake with gastric reflux, and spend hours propped up on pillows. I drift off to sleep then wake wide-eyed thirty minutes later. During nights of insomnia, I picture Steve in his hospital bed. Is he comfortable? Does he wake every time the nurses turn him? I toss restlessly until the panic subsides and my eyes become heavy.

*

April 2016. There is a baby on the way – our first grandchild. I remind Steve regularly that a little one is coming.

One day when Sally visits, I place his hand on her growing belly. 'There's a baby in there,' I tell him.

'Isn't it amazing?' Steve smiles.

*

May 2016. The battery in Steve's pacemaker is replaced. It's a simple procedure that occurs every two to three years and we follow the usual protocol – two nights in North Shore Private Hospital, twenty-four hours intravenous antibiotics and home again. Before discharge, the nurse takes photos of Steve's chest. It looks red and swollen where the battery has been inserted but she assures me the swelling will go down over time.

Ten days later, blood trickles from the wound. It snakes its way down his chest, a dark, thin line that stains his white T-shirt. A nurse at the facility cleans the wound and applies a new bandage. Steve's chest looks bruised and reddened around the wound but the suture line appears clean and seems to be healing.

On a Sunday night two and a half weeks following surgery, I walk into the facility to help Steve with his dinner and see that his wound has bled again. The front of his green T-shirt is saturated in rich, dark blood. He looks as though he's been in a massacre, stabbed repeatedly in the chest. A nurse is called to check the source of the bleeding and finds a tiny split in the suture line. She reassures me there is no sign of infection, but I know this is not normal. The next morning, I ring the

Parkinson's nurse and an appointment is organised with the neurosurgeon in Sydney for the following day.

The doctor palpates Steve's chest and blood oozes profusely from the wound. He diagnoses a haematoma and says he will have to operate to release the built-up fluid. When I ask if Steve's chest is infected, he remains non-committal. He won't know until he operates. Surgery is scheduled for late the following day.

Steve has an infection. The doctor suspects the bacteria has come from a urinary tract infection, probably present at the time of his battery replacement. Steve wears a compression bandage to reduce the risk of swelling in his chest and begins fourteen days of intravenous antibiotics.

I book a motel room in Sydney so that I can spend the days with Steve and help him with his recovery. When the loneliness and stress of my vigil become too much, I allow myself rest days at home or commute to the hospital from Newcastle. I take a survival kit with me to pass the time: some knitting for the expected baby, crossword books, my iPad.

At the end of two weeks, the microbiologist puts Steve on two types of oral antibiotics – large white horse pills – that are intended to control the infection that clings to the foreign device in Steve's chest. He will take these antibiotics for the rest of his life.

*

18 August 2016. Sally's son is born. I am privileged to be present at his birth, to witness his first breath. At six thirty p.m. I leave the labour ward and drive to the aged care facility. I'm excited to tell Steve about his grandson's arrival, the miracle of his birth. When I arrive at the facility, Steve is already in bed, but still awake. I prop him up and show him a photo of Sally and the baby. I wonder if he'll understand the magnitude of this occasion but my doubts are unfounded.

'Isn't it great!' he beams.

Sally and Aaron name their little boy Nathaniel Stephen.

*

November 2016. Steve deteriorates suddenly. He becomes immobile. The food placed in his mouth dribbles out. He can't suck on a straw. His medications need to be crushed.

I try to check the DBS battery in his pacemaker with the patient programmer and am unable to get a reading. A big X appears on the screen. It is a weekend, so I ring the emergency number for the battery manufacturer. I am advised by one technician that the symbol on the programmer means the battery is flat. He passes me onto another colleague, who assures me the battery isn't flat. He suggests the therapy controller may not be compatible with the device and recommends trying a different one. When the Parkinson's nurse visits the next day with her more sophisticated programmer, she also cannot get a reading. She suspects Steve's battery has flipped over during a fall and this is the reason we cannot communicate with the device. She examines Steve and assures me that the battery must still be working or his condition would be far worse. She rings the nurse in Sydney who liaises with Steve's neurosurgeon. She will ring me when she has spoken to the doctor.

Three days pass. My phone calls and messages to the nurse in Sydney go unanswered. Steve has now been immobile for a week. The nurses at the home say he lies rigid in the bed at night. He barely eats but manages fluids and medications. He is sometimes able to walk with two nurses attending. The Sydney nurse finally contacts me and says the doctors are reluctant to do anything without an assessment from Steve's neurologist in Newcastle. An appointment is organised for the following day, with an X-ray of Steve's chest also booked in.

Steve sits slouched in his wheelchair while we wait for the doctor. Katie and Steve's sister, Lynette, have come with me to the appointment. The neurologist examines Steve and then sends him for the X-ray to assess the position of the battery. While Steve is away, the doctor speaks to Katie and me. He is a quietly spoken, considerate man, about our age and has been Steve's doctor for thirteen years. He gently suggests that Steve's worsening condition may be due to the progression of his

Parkinson's. He feels that more parts of Steve's brain are involved in his illness now. He asks us to consider end of life protocols. Should we put Steve through a barrage of tests in hospital to determine the exact nature of his deterioration? Should we insert a peg feed if Steve is no longer able to eat? What do we want for Steve? I have been expecting this conversation, but Katie sits beside me in tears. I acknowledge the points the doctor raises; perhaps Steve is nearing the end.

I tell the doctor I want Steve to be kept comfortable, but as we prepare to leave I look him in the eye and say, 'Don't be surprised if he doesn't bounce back from this.'

The next day, Steve's neurosurgeon and neurologist attend a conference in Newcastle. The timing is purely coincidental but fortuitous for Steve, as it provides an opportunity for both Sydney and Newcastle doctors to discuss his situation. A representative from the battery manufacturer is also present. He comes to visit Steve in the aged care facility to check the device. He, too, assures me that the battery is working but has most likely flipped over in his chest when he has fallen. When I don't hear back from the doctors or nurses, I presume no further action will be taken. Clearly, everyone is convinced that the battery is working and Steve's deterioration is due to his illness.

The conference takes place on a Friday. On the following Monday afternoon, I receive a phone call from the Parkinson's nurse in Sydney. Can I bring Steve down for surgery on Thursday? The doctors have decided to operate to turn the battery over and check its status. I am flummoxed; I express my concerns. Why put Steve through another surgery if the battery is working anyway? She tells me no one has a crystal ball. Steve's condition has worsened and although the battery doesn't appear damaged, it's impossible to say with any certainty where the problem lies.

I agonise over this decision. I don't want to put Steve through any unnecessary treatment. Another anaesthetic and the risk of infection on the already compromised chest area are a concern. The logistics of the trip to Sydney also seem formidable. But Steve is deteriorating. He has lost five kilos. He is unable to communicate with us. He is now the zombie he once so feared becoming. If we do nothing, he will not survive. What do we have to lose? Later, I learn that the doctors, too, were undecided. Steve's medical history was so complex, difficult and problematic. So much had gone wrong with all his previous surgeries and treatments. Perhaps they felt that he'd been through enough. Still, an element of doubt overshadowed their decision – the possibility that there was something wrong with the battery, something that could be fixed.

On Thursday morning, I drive Steve to North Shore Private Hospital. Katie and Lynette accompany us while Sally waits anxiously at home with her new son. The admissions staff quickly usher us into a cubicle to await surgery. I have requested a meeting with the neurosurgeon before the operation and he visits us in his scrubs. He examines Steve's chest and tries, unsuccessfully, to manually turn the battery over. He seems genuinely concerned and empathetic over Steve's condition and tries to reassure me that this will be a simple procedure. His tone is encouraging and, as always, confident.

The doctor and Parkinson's nurse enter Steve's room after surgery.

'We've put a new battery in,' the nurse tells us. 'We couldn't communicate with the old one either.'

It takes me a moment to process this news.

The doctor seems just as surprised by this outcome. 'We don't know if the battery was faulty or whether Steve damaged it when he fell,' he offers. The old battery will be sent to the manufacturer for testing.

When Steve comes back from recovery, I can see the improvement immediately. His face has a smooth, relaxed look, the tension from the previous two weeks erased from his features. When I offer him some ice from a cup, he crunches it down; he swallows his tablets effortlessly. The next day when I arrive at the hospital, Steve is sitting up in bed. He smiles as I enter the room and jokes with Katie.

Later, when the neurosurgeon visits we both marvel at the difference in Steve. 'It's a miracle,' I say, and the doctor's face creases into a broad smile.

*

May 2017. I crack the egg into the bowl. The hand-held mixer whisks the egg and then I add cream, milk, and sugar. I add the flour then knead the scone dough, cut rounds and brush each round with milk. When I take them out of the oven, the kitchen is filled with their sweet smell. I leave the scones cooling on a wire rack, a clean tea towel draped over their golden tops, ready for a neighbourhood high tea later this afternoon.

At one p.m., Steve falls on the concrete path at the nursing home. He has been falling frequently, with dramatic drops in his blood pressure. He lands face first. Blood pours from two wounds – a deep gash above his left eye and a split between his mouth and nose. The nurses turn him on his side as he begins to retch and choke on his own blood.

I run from him. I cannot witness his damaged face, his crumpled body lying on the ground. I hide in a corner of the garden. I feel dizzy, sick, faint. A nurse brings me a drink of water and I sip tiny mouthfuls. Tears stream down my face.

'How much more can we deal with?' I wail.

The nurse speaks softly. 'It's a terrible disease,' she sympathises. 'Neither of you should have to go through this.'

I feel guilty because I was at the home with him and should have prevented his fall but the nurse shakes her head. 'You're up against the elements.'

The ambulance arrives to take Steve to hospital.

The paramedic takes one look at him and says, 'Mr Boulton! He used to teach me.' She left school in the late 80s but still remembered Steve as her favourite teacher. The trip to hospital is filled with stories of her schooldays and the many ways in which Steve had helped her.

The doctor at the hospital cleans Steve's wounds and glues the lacerations together. She is a beautiful young African doctor, her hair a mass of tight braids. Steve keeps trying to climb off the bed. He is responding now and becoming agitated. I breathe more easily – he is back to his 'normal' self. The doctor says a CT scan of Steve's head is required to see if he has had a brain bleed. He would require sedation, as the test takes some twenty minutes, and we all know he won't stay still. The doctor goes away to consult with her superior. The scan is cancelled. Even if they find a problem, they wouldn't treat it because of Steve's condition. He is moved from casualty to a short-stay unit while we wait for patient transport to take us back to the facility. The nurses in the short-stay ward are kind and caring. One of them mumbles something about 'loyalty' and her concern for me is beyond comforting.

I cannot stop crying. I am exhausted and despondent. I am also angry at Steve. I've missed the afternoon tea – a rare social occasion I've been looking forward to for weeks. Steve's injuries are upsetting but I'm resentful. How dare he fall today of all days! Why do I always have to miss out? I can never relax and enjoy myself. When will this ever end?

I walk into the kitchen. It is nine p.m. and Steve is safely in bed at the nursing home. I put a piece of bread in the toaster for my dinner. The scones are still sitting on the bench. I lift the tea towel, take the rack over to the garbage bin and throw them away.

*

The late 1970s. Scene: a suburban ballet studio. A male and female aged early twenties.

The studio is an old scout hall with unlined walls and particle board flooring. A cold wind whistles through the cracks in the walls, a small bar heater doing little to alleviate the winter chill. An old refrigerator and a metal garbage bin, the lid askew, stand against one wall. Long wooden benches are pushed up against another.

The girl wears a black leotard and hand-knitted blue leg warmers. The boy wears black tights and a navy blue T-shirt, his long curly hair pulled back in a pony-tail. Despite the cold, beads of sweat glisten on their brows.

They are practising the white swan *pas de deux* from the ballet *Swan Lake*. This has been her dream since childhood – to be the swan queen. He has been dancing for only a few years but is talented and ambitious.

From the old tape recorder in the corner of the room come the haunting strains of Tchaikovsky's famous music.

Her arms fluttering, his arms protectively around her, the swan queen and her prince profess their undying love for each other. Their bodies move in unison, entwining and unravelling until they reach the final pose.

*

14 June 2017. Steve dies. Suddenly, unexpectedly, inexplicably, alone.

When I arrive at the facility, the nurses meet me at the door, crying. I am led to his room. He is lying on the bed, his long, lean frame stretched out, his head tilted slightly to one side. His mouth is open and I can see one cloudy eye in the space between his semi-closed eyelids. His face has taken on the yellowish hue of death. I kiss his cool forehead and close his eye. I reach under the quilt and hold his hand. It is still warm. Over the next few hours, I clutch desperately at his hand, willing it to stay warm. It still feels like Steve but when I try to kiss his open lips they feel cold and lifeless.

I have no tears.

Six days later, I see Steve in his coffin at the funeral home. He looks peaceful. His face is pale and waxy, his skin smooth, his grey curls freshly brushed, his lips pressed together. I touch his chest. The familiar bulge of the pacemaker is gone. His hands are folded together on his stomach and I slip my fingers into his. Icy.

I cry. I want to take him home

*

21 June 2017. Steve's funeral. I stand at the microphone to deliver the eulogy. I do not falter. I am not nervous. My tribute to Steve is heartfelt but I speak calmly. I am strangely detached from the enormity of this occasion. It feels like a performance. Surreal. I do not make eye contact with anyone. The chapel is filled to capacity and there are people sitting

and standing in the outdoor area. I want to scream at this faceless crowd, 'Where were you?' When I sit down after the eulogy, I begin to shake and cannot stop.

I show a small video clip of Steve and me dancing. It was filmed in 1996, five years before his Parkinson's diagnosis. We are in our early forties and out of practice but the dance flows with movement, music, and love. The 'audience' around me erupts with thunderous applause.

Our final *pas de deux*.

Curtain Call

In the weeks and months following Steve's death, I look for distractions. I keep busy. I avoid being at home. I cannot bear the twilight hours, the encroaching darkness, the prospect of cooking and eating a lonely meal, or the afternoon quiz shows on television. They remind me of time spent with Steve in his room after dinner when he dozed in his chair and I passed the time with crosswords while we waited for bedtime. The freedom I'd once yearned for stretches before me, uninvitingly.

My friends regularly invite me out for coffees. I join a walking group. I return to my weekly ballet class. I make a point of never refusing a social invitation but after every outing I return, alone, to my empty house. In time my friends, understandably, resume their own lives and the ensuing silence overwhelms me. Nothing fills the emptiness and the days roll on without purpose. It takes all my energy and reserves to keep breathing and to just be present. When I wake, I walk aimlessly through the house, dreading the day ahead. What do I do now? How do I fill in my time? Who am I now?

Most mornings, Archie looks at me expectantly through the family room window so I attach his lead and take him for a walk. The fresh air and attention to my dog seem to clear my head. Sometimes, I meet other walkers who stop for a chat. This simple interaction eases my loneliness and replenishes my desperate need for human contact.

I have flashbacks – Steve, lifeless on the bed, in ICU following brain surgery, looking pleadingly at me as his Parkinson's symptoms render him helpless and immobile. I liken the flashbacks to a kaleidoscope, alighting in a different place every time, never knowing where the images will settle. The years Steve spent in care blur and become strangely indistinguishable, without substance, blanked from my memory. I hated having him in the facility and the constant visiting. I hated the guilt, grief, stress and resentment over his illness and his incarceration. Now I long for the familiarity and routine of those days and wish he was still there. Yet, every night, when I kiss his photo, I see the ravages of his illness and cannot wish him back.

Grief ebbs and flows. Powerful emotions are never far from the surface. And disbelief. How can he be dead? How could this have happened so swiftly? I'd expected some warning – perhaps a serious fall or a worsening of his Parkinson's symptoms. Not this sudden parting with no answers and no goodbye. But there is relief, too, that his suffering is over, and that the end was mercifully quick.

I am unprepared for the loneliness. Or for how much I miss Steve. Although we had not lived in the same home for over three years nor shared the emotional and physical intimacies of husband and wife, I still depended on him. Despite Steve's incapacity, I'd always confided in him and found comfort in his presence. Now I miss his companionship, however limited, and long for his hugs. After years of staying strong for Steve, of being the decision-maker, of having some measure of control, I become suddenly needy and vulnerable, unsure of myself, or of my future. My life feels meaningless without him by my side.

Five weeks after Steve's death, when the financial practicalities of my newly acquired widowhood overwhelm me, I rage at him. How could you leave me to deal with this on my own? A counsellor tells me that this is often the worst period of mourning, when the bereaved must deal with the legal requirements of a death. She reminds me that life will get better, but my chest tightens and I feel a rising panic every time I think of Steve and the prospect of the rest of my life without him.

Eventually, I return to the nursing home. My heart pounds as I follow the familiar road I've driven twice daily for more than three years. My anxiety intensifies when I walk through the locked gate and into the home. I feel closer to Steve when I am there and the nurses, who have become my friends, welcome me fondly; I've missed them. Steve's blue recliner chair is positioned in the dining room and another resident is benefiting from my donation. She reminds me of Steve with her stooped posture and incessant need to bend over to touch and examine everything.

I stay in the communal areas. I cannot bear to walk down the long corridor that leads to Steve's room. An elderly man lives there now and a new name graces the bedroom door. When I see the residents sitting in the lounge room, I wonder which chair Steve was in when he passed away. Did he know he was about to die? What happened in those last moments? Could I have prevented his death if I'd been there? How could I have been shopping and not known that my husband was dying? After all my years of vigilance, love and devotion, I was absent when he needed me most.

I replay that final day over and over. I was late getting to the nursing home – I had an early appointment and a carer would be giving him his lunch, so I took the rare opportunity to relax and have a leisurely meal at home. I can't remember if I gave Steve a kiss when I came in. Did I tell him I loved him? We joined in an activity, a ball game. Steve enjoyed throwing and catching the ball. I remember his cheeky grin as he teased the other residents with his still agile ball skills. Later, he had some afternoon tea and we walked in the sun-filled garden. It was a warm winter afternoon. I held his hand tightly. I left just before three p.m. for a dental appointment. I settled him in a chair with a biscuit. I never said goodbye after my afternoon visit, as I worried he would want to come with me or become upset at my leaving. Instead, one of the nurses would often distract him as I quietly slipped away. I would be back at five, to help him with his dinner, and to spend time with him before helping him into bed at seven.

The nurses found him in his chair, *The Sound of Music* playing on the large TV screen in the background.

The phone call came just before four p.m.

*

October 2017. My neighbour dreams of Steve. He has a message for me: 'Tell Linda I'm happy. Tell her not to worry – everything will be all right.' In the dream, Steve looks healthy with no sign of Parkinson's.

Soon after, a friend whom I haven't seen for some time speaks to a medium in a spiritualist church. The medium says a man with grey, curly hair is standing before her. My friend recognises Steve. He is looking sad. 'He says he's sorry he didn't get a chance to say goodbye,' she reveals.

I'm comforted by these messages. Later, I realise they coincide with Steve's sixty-third birthday.

*

December 2017. Archie is dying. His diagnosis of a rare form of lymphoma just two months after Steve's death crushes us all. My loyal walking buddy gradually succumbs to festering skin lesions. His once voracious appetite is quelled. When we walk our familiar path, he turns back, exhausted, just metres from home. In the final weeks, his body exudes an unpleasant odour and I smell his imminent death.

On Christmas morning, Archie circles our backyard looking for a place to rest. He can no longer climb the stairs to the veranda to the comfort of his kennel and bed. When the family arrives for dinner, he rallies enough to join us, sleeping on the lounge room rug. He's been part of our family for exactly ten years.

Katie opens the veterinary clinic on Boxing Day and prepares to euthanise our beloved pet. The syringe is drawn up, the body bag ready. She lifts Archie up onto the examination table, shaves his forearm and gently injects the lethal fluid into his veins. He is gone within seconds and I am distraught. My grief over my pet seems almost indecent, somehow. How can I grieve so openly over Archie's death, yet barely shed a tear over Steve's? What sort of wife am I? Sally reminds me there are different ways of grieving.

Later, Katie has Archie cremated and his ashes join Steve's at home.

*

January 2018. I've come back to Hawks Nest, Steve's favourite holiday destination, to visit our friends who still camp here. I welcome the familiarity of the area and memories of happier times, but I feel Steve's absence keenly. Sally and Aaron join me, eager to introduce little Nathaniel to our holiday tradition of camping, surf and sun. The next generation of campers is growing – two new grandchildren will join our family this year.

After lunch, we head to the bay for a swim. The crystal-blue waters of Port Stephens sparkle in the sunlight. The dual headlands of Tomaree and Yacaaba guard the entrance to the bay. Waves crash against their rocky bases. In the distance, a pod of dolphins surfaces briefly before dipping back down into the blue depths of the bay. A pelican sails serenely in the shallow waters close to shore.

Seventeen-month-old Nathaniel chases seagulls, tottering on unsteady legs in the soft sand. He ploughs on determinedly, undeterred by the birds' rapid flight when he approaches. I hold his hand and we walk to the water's edge, where the cold waves lap at his tiny feet. Nathaniel sucks in his breath and reaches both arms up to be held. His sweet upturned face looks at me trustingly. I lift him up onto my hip and he snuggles in my arms contentedly. We stand together, gazing out past the headlands to the open ocean beyond.

Acknowledgements

I am indebted to the following for their invaluable contribution to the writing of this memoir.

I would like to thank my supervisors at the University of Newcastle for their unwavering belief in me. I am forever grateful to Associate Professor Keri Glastonbury for her encouragement and support and for giving me the confidence to write my story. She counselled the writing of this memoir with unfailing wisdom, knowledge, and compassion. I also express my gratitude to Associate Professor Jesper Gulddal for his guidance, encouragement and critical appraisal of my work.

I want to thank Cassandra O'Loughlin for her mentoring and close reading of my manuscript. I am grateful, too, to Sally Hoyle and Supatra Gill for their feedback on early drafts of this memoir.

My appreciation goes to Stephen Matthews OAM at Ginninderra Press for his advice and assistance and for giving me the opportunity to see my book in print. This publication will help raise the profile of family caregivers and shine a light on the vital support they provide.

Acknowledgements are due to Abigail Thomas, *A Three Dog Life: A Memoir*, New York, Harcourt, 2006; and Joel Havemann, *A Life Shaken: My Encounter with Parkinson's Disease*, Baltimore, John Hopkins UP, 2002.

Excerpts from this memoir have been published in *Humanities*, 2013, 'Illness Narratives: The Carer Memoir', and *The Lifted Brow, The Medicine Issue*, 2014, 'He didn't even have a tremor: A Parkinson's Pathography'.

Thank you to my home cheer squad for your faith in me. Your love and support helped me through the dark times. I especially want to thank my beautiful daughters Sally and Katie, who are always there for me, and my gorgeous grandchildren Nathaniel, Sebastian, Ava and Josephine, who always give me a reason to smile.

Finally, and most importantly, my heartfelt thanks go to Steve, who allowed me to share our story. He is my inspiration and will always be the love of my life.

www.ingramcontent.com/pod-product-compliance
Lightning Source LLC
Chambersburg PA
CBHW030909080526
44589CB00010B/211